The Best Stage Scenes of 2000

Other books by Jocelyn A. Beard

Smith and Kraus *Books For Actors*

YOUNG ACTOR SERIES

Great Scenes and Monologues For Children Volumes I and II

Forensics Duo Series for Young Actors Volume I: 35 8 to 10-Minute Original Comedic
    Scenes for Duo Practice and Performance

Forensics Duo Series for Young Actors Volume II: 35 8 to 10-Minute Original
    Dramatic Scenes for Duo Practice and Performance

Great Scenes In Dialect for Young Actors

Great Scenes For Young Actors Volumes I and II

Monologues and Scenes For Middle School Actors

Multicultural Scenes For Young Actors

SCENE STUDY SERIES

The Best Stage Scenes Of 1999

The Best Stage Scenes Of 1998

The Best Stage Scenes Of 1997

The Best Stage Scenes Of 1996

The Best Stage Scenes Of 1995

The Best Stage Scenes Of 1994

The Best Stage Scenes Of 1993

The Best Stage Scenes Of 1992

The Best Stage Scenes For Men From the 1980s

The Best Stage Scenes For Women From the 1980s

The Ultimate Scene Study Series Volume I: 101 Short Scenes for Groups

The Ultimate Scene Study Series Volume II: 102 Short Scenes for Two Actors

The Ultimate Scene Study Series Volume III: 103 Short Scenes for Three Actors

The Ultimate Scene Study Series Volume IV: 104 Short Scenes for Four Actors

Kiss and Tell—Restoration Comedy of Manners: Scenes, Monologues and
    Historical Context

A Brave and Violent Theatre Monologues, Scenes and Historical Context for 20th
    Century Irish Drama

Scenes From Classic Plays 468 B.C. To 1970 A.D.

If you require pre-publication information about upcoming Smith and Kraus books, you may receive our semi-annual catalogue, free of charge, by sending your name and address to *Smith and Kraus Catalogue, 4 Lower Mill Road, North Stratford, NH 03590. Or call us at (800) 895-4331, fax (603) 643-6431.*

The Best
Stage Scenes
of 2000

edited by Jocelyn A. Beard

SCENE STUDY SERIES

A SMITH AND KRAUS BOOK

Published by Smith and Kraus, Inc.
177 Lyme Road, Hanover, NH 03755
www.SmithKraus.com

Copyright © 2002 by Smith and Kraus, Inc.
All rights reserved
Manufactured in the United States of America

First Edition: May 2002
10 9 8 7 6 5 4 3 2 1

cover illustration by Lisa Goldfinger
cover design by Julia Hill Gignoux

The Scene Study Series 1067-3253
ISBN 1-57525-289-9

CONTENTS

SCENES FOR MEN AND WOMEN

SCENES FOR MEN

SCENES FOR WOMEN

Dedicated to the Victims of September 11, 2001

Scenes for Men and Women

APARTMENT 3A
Jeff Daniels
2 Men 1 Woman

Scene: An apartment in a city of some size in the Midwest.

Annie (thirties), a woman struggling to cope with the loss of what she thought was the love of her life, and Elliot (thirties), a co-worker who falls in love with her.

Annie, a self-proclaimed atheist, is shocked to discover that her friend and co-worker is Catholic. Here, they debate spiritual matters over lunch.

DONALD: So he's Catholic? So what?

ANNIE: If I'd have been smart, I'd have said, "Look, this was a bad idea. Let's just go back to the station and everybody lives happily ever after." But no, not me.

DONALD: Simply because he's Catholic?

ANNIE: No, because it came up in conversation.

DONALD: What did?

ANNIE: His being Catholic.

DONALD: Why? What did you say?

ANNIE: I didn't say anything. It was him. He's the one who said it. *(Elliot turns to Annie.)*

ELLIOT: I'm Catholic. *(Annie looks at Donald.)*

DONALD: Maybe he was just trying to make conversation.

ANNIE: Well, that's what I thought. I'm thinking okay, he's nervous, he's already spent an unusual amount of time in the men's room doing God knows what, he's just lobbied unsuccessfully for dinner and now, to keep things moving forward, he decides to come out of the closet about his religious convictions. Just making conversation. *(Elliot repeats the identical moment.)*

ELLIOT: I'm Catholic.

DONALD: I still don't see why that's such a disaster.

ANNIE: You don't say something like that to someone over lunch. If you're

going to make an announcement like that, if you're going to reveal intimate details about yourself that—

DONALD: What did you say?

ANNIE: —in hindsight, would have been nice for the person who's hearing it
to have, perhaps, known it was coming ahead of time, you should by all
means, y'know . . .

DONALD: Send up a flare?

ANNIE: Send up a flare! Exactly! It's common luncheon courtesy!

DONALD: So what did you say? *(Annie hangs her head.)* Annie?
(Elliot repeats the identical moment.)

ELLIOT: I'm Catholic.

ANNIE: Oh. Well, in that case, you should probably know I don't believe in
God. *(Elliot sits there, stunned. Annie turns to Donald.)* It just came out.
I didn't plan it. I didn't even know I felt that way. I'd never thought
about it really. That's not true. I've thought about it a lot. I'd just never
said it. Out loud. I don't believe in God.

DONALD: It's all right.

ANNIE: Yeah, it's all right. Everything's all right. Hey, like it matters what I
think, right? . . . Right?

DONALD: Right.

ANNIE: Tell him that.

ELLIOT: You what?

ANNIE: I'd ask if you do, but that would be a stupid question, wouldn't it?

ELLIOT: I don't believe this.

ANNIE: Yeah well, that makes two of us.

ELLIOT: Why?

ANNIE: Why what?

ELLIOT: Why don't you believe in God?

ANNIE: Because I don't.

ELLIOT: I'm . . . I'm stunned.

ANNIE: Well, you're the one who wanted to go to lunch.

ELLIOT: I know, but I didn't know you were . . .

ANNIE: "I'm Catholic?" What did you expect me to say?

ELLIOT: Lent.

ANNIE: Lent?

ELLIOT: It's Lent. I'm giving up pasta for Lent. That's why I ordered the eggs.
That's why I told you I was Catholic.

ANNIE: Oh. I thought you were just making conversation.

ELLIOT: Just making conversation?

ANNIE: Well, how was I supposed to know?

ELLIOT: This is a lunch! We're having lunch! You don't—

ANNIE: I know that.

ELLIOT: —talk about the existence of God over lunch!

ANNIE: Well fine, let's talk about something else. I don't care.

ELLIOT: We can't talk about something else! Not now!

ANNIE: Fine! So let's talk about it!

  (Pause.)

ELLIOT: So. You're an atheist.

ANNIE: No, I'm not.

DONALD: Liar.

ANNIE: *(To Donald.)* I'm not!

ELLIOT: You just said you didn't believe in God.

ANNIE: I don't not believe. I'm willing to believe. I just need, y'know, a little
  bit more, I don't know . . .

ELLIOT: Proof?

ANNIE: Proof. Yes. Proof would be nice.

ELLIOT: Like what, some miracle? Maybe the Second Coming? Would the
  Second Coming do it for you?

ANNIE: You can lose the attitude, Elliot. You're the one who wanted to talk
  religion.

ELLIOT: I'm sorry, I'm just . . . I'm completely at a loss here.

ANNIE: Yeah well, get in line.

ELLIOT: What about something smaller?

ANNIE: Something smaller than the Second Coming?

ELLIOT: Y'know, some everyday thing we take for granted that's inexplicable,
  that can't be accounted for but could be construed as a miracle.

ANNIE: I don't believe in miracles.

ELLIOT: You don't believe in . . .

ANNIE: I believe if we ever see a waiter that would be a miracle. How's that?
  Is that acceptable? Can we get off of me now?

ELLIOT: Fine.

ANNIE: Fine! *(Pause.)* What about you?

ELLIOT: What about me?

ANNIE: Why do you believe in God?

ELLIOT: I'm Catholic.

ANNIE: Yes, I know. But why do you believe?

ELLIOT: No, that's why.

ANNIE: That's why you believe?

ELLIOT: Yes.

ANNIE: Okay. But even though you're Catholic, you've had doubts.

ELLIOT: About what?

ANNIE: About the possibility of a Godless existence?

ELLIOT: Never.

DONALD: Liar.

ANNIE: You've always believed there was a God.

ELLIOT: Absolutely.

ANNIE: Based on what?

ELLIOT: Based on the fact that I'm Catholic.

ANNIE: That's not a reason.

ELLIOT: It's a good enough reason for me.

ANNIE: Elliot, that's like saying you believe in chocolate because there's a Hershey's plant in Pennsylvania.

ELLIOT: There is a Hershey's plant in Pennsylvania.

ANNIE: You're missing the point.

ELLIOT: There's also such a thing as chocolate.

ANNIE: Fine. Look. Forget you're Catholic for a second.

ELLIOT: Forget I'm Catholic?

ANNIE: Yes.

ELLIOT: I can't forget I'm Catholic. It's ingrained, imbedded—

ANNIE: Just try.

ELLIOT: —it's tattooed on my soul.

ANNIE: Why do you, Elliot Brown, the person, the individual, the human being, believe without a doubt, no questions asked, one hundred percent guaranteed, that there is a God?

ELLIOT: Listen, if you'd gotten whacked on the back of the head by Sister Mary Bernice as many times as I did, you'd believe there was a God, too.

ANNIE: So you believe out of fear.

ELLIOT: It wasn't fear.

ANNIE: A woman dressed in black beat you in the name of the Father, Son and Holy Ghost, Elliot. Don't tell me it wasn't fear.

ELLIOT: Okay, technically, there was some fear.

ANNIE: And out of that fear, you never once thought there might not be a God?

ELLIOT: No.

ANNIE: Not once.

ELLIOT: Never. Never crossed my mind. It's not even crossing my mind now.

ANNIE: Carl Sagan? Stephen Hawking? Ever heard them talk about God?

ELLIOT: Carl Sagan and—

ANNIE: The answer is—

ELLIOT: —Stephen Hawking?

ANNIE: —no, you haven't because they don't. They avoid the subject completely.

ELLIOT: Just because they don't talk about it—

ANNIE: And what about NASA?

ELLIOT: NASA? What's NASA got to do with—

ANNIE: All those satellites and nuclear-powered telescopes on all those California mountain tops pointed towards the heavens, beaming back pictures from every corner of the galaxy and nowhere, not in one photograph that's come back has there ever been anything remotely resembling something that could possibly pass for God?

ELLIOT: I think you're putting far too much faith in a federal agency.

ANNIE: Am I?

ELLIOT: Yes.

ANNIE: You don't think they want to find it?

ELLIOT: I don't have the faintest idea what they want.

ANNIE: Okay then. What about Houdini?

ELLIOT: The magician?

ANNIE: He made a pledge.

ELLIOT: To the station?

ANNIE: No. He's dead. Houdini's been—

ELLIOT: That's what—

ANNIE: —dead for year.

ELLIOT: —I thought, that's why I, y'know.

ANNIE: True story. On his deathbed, Houdini made this promise. One last trick, as it were. He told his wife that one year after he died, on the following Halloween night, he wanted her to gather all of his closest friends right there in that very same room and hold a seance. And during that seance, if there truly were an afterlife, a heaven, a God of any kind, he would come to them. Proving it was so. Well, guess what? They're still waiting.

ELLIOT: That doesn't prove anything.

ANNIE: No, but it doesn't help, does it?

ELLIOT: Maybe God wasn't a big Houdini fan.

ANNIE: All right, then what about this? Tell me why Jesus was born.

ELLIOT: Why?

ANNIE: Yes, and don't go off on the Immaculate Conception because I don't even want to get into that. All I want to know is why you think he was born.

ELLIOT: Because God so loved the world he gave—

ANNIE: Don't quote the Bible. I don't want the Bible. I'm asking you. Why do you, Elliot, think Jesus was brought into this world?

ELLIOT: To bring the message of God to the people.

ANNIE: Why?

ELLIOT: To spread the word of God.

ANNIE: Why?

ELLIOT: Because they needed to hear it.

ANNIE: Because why?

ELLIOT: Because they were a bunch of fuckups! *(Elliot whips his head around to see if anyone overheard him.)*

ANNIE: Exactly! Okay. The whole world was full of fuckups. Everywhere you looked there was chaos. Tyranny, genocide, starvation, disease, power, greed, corruption, wars, no morals, no values, no sense of right and wrong—they were barbaric times, right?

ELLIOT: Right.

ANNIE: So God sent Jesus to show them the way.

ELLIOT: Yes.

ANNIE: So what's changed? Two thousand years later and what's different? Except for technology, everywhere you look it's still the same as it was then. I turn on the evening news and I watch a three-year-old Bosnian girl, nude from the waist down, shitting herself to death in the mud and snow. I listen to yet another team of investigators tell me about another black box discovered in yet another airplane that blew up all in the name of somebody's idea of religion.

ELLIOT: Religion is—

ANNIE: I watch live reports about death from Oklahoma City, Atlanta, Beirut,

Belfast, Sarajevo, Kosovo, Somalia, Romania, Tiananmen Square, Chechnya, Jerusalem—Jerusalem! Forty-five kids are gunned down in a San Diego McDonald's. Two days later it's Texas. Five years later it's Columbine. Pick a city. Pick a town. Pick the place where somebody'll snap next week.

ELLIOT: Annie.

ANNIE: AIDS, leukemia, cancer, racism, fascism, sexism. If you're poor, you're lazy. If you're raped, you asked for it. Hatred overwhelms love. Greed wins out over compassion and meanwhile, our own Christian based government is either going to war or sponsoring one, not to fight for freedom but because it's good for business because there's lots of money to be made when other people die, by God. And to comfort us, all we have to soothe us, to make everything okay again is an 800 number we can call to talk to someone—

ELLIOT: That's not even fair—

ANNIE: —who will pray for us in Jesus' name so long as we support the right political party! That's why I wonder. That's why I question whether there truly is a God. Because if He came then, why isn't He coming now? *(Pause.)*

ELLIOT: If He came back now, it would mean we failed. We didn't learn anything.

ANNIE: Well, maybe we know too much.

ELLIOT: Maybe. And maybe we don't know as much as we think. Besides, it would be too late.

ANNIE: Too late for what?

ELLIOT: For you.

ANNIE: For me?

ELLIOT: There's no use saying you believe in Him after He's come back, after —

ANNIE: I don't believe in Him, Elliot.

ELLIOT: —He's, I know—

ANNIE: Today. Tomorrow. Ever.

ELLIOT: —I know, you told me, you told me already. But, y'know, all I'm saying is, what if you're wrong? *(Off Annie's reaction.)* No, what if you're wrong and He does come back? Or something happens that tells you? Y'know, provides proof?
(Donald sketches.)

DONALD: Being in the right place at the right time.

ELLIOT: That shows us that this whole natural universe we thought we knew is merely a step to something else. Something so beautiful, it's inconceivable.

DONALD: Love at first sight.

ELLIOT: So beyond what we think we know to be true.

DONALD: Finding something you thought was lost forever.

ELLIOT: Something maybe we aren't supposed to understand.

ANNIE: *(To Donald.)* Lost what?

DONALD: I'm just thinking. Maybe Houdini had the right idea, but just went about it in the wrong way.

ANNIE: Are you Catholic, too?

DONALD: No. I prefer to put my money into mutual funds.

ANNIE: But you believe in God.

DONALD: I believe there is no way on earth I possess that talent necessary to paint my wife that day. But I did.

ANNIE: Maybe it was Houdini.

DONALD: Yes. Maybe it was Houdini. *(Donald holds Annie with a look.)*

ELLIOT: What if you're right? What if Houdini had come back and proved you were right? "I've come back and I'm here to tell you, there is no afterlife. There's no God. There's no heaven. There's nothing. Jesus Christ was just a carpenter's son with a lot of good ideas." Would you really want to know that?

DONALD: Would you?

ANNIE: I don't know what I want to know anymore.

BACK STORY
"Norman Rockwell's Thanksgiving in the Year 2000"
Joan Ackermann
Man & Woman

Scene: Here and now.

Ethan and Ainsley (eighteen to twenty), brother and sister doing their best to survive in a fractured family.

Here, Ethan and Ainsley compose a Thanksgiving letter to their estranged father.

ETHAN: *(Earnestly.)* Read it again.

AINSLEY: Did you just fart?

ETHAN: No.

AINSLEY: You did.

ETHAN: I didn't.

AINSLEY: You did.

ETHAN: Well. It's Thanksgiving.

AINSLEY: Oh right.

ETHAN: Read it again.

AINSLEY: "Dear Jim . . ."

ETHAN: Maybe we should say . . . "Dear Dad."

AINSLEY: We never do.

ETHAN: We don't?

AINSLEY: No.

ETHAN: Oh.

AINSLEY: "Dear Jim . . ."

ETHAN: We never write to him.
  (She looks at him.)

ETHAN: So we never write "Dear Jim" or "Dear Dad."

AINSLEY: We've written to him.

ETHAN: When?

AINSLEY: Ethan . . .

ETHAN: I think we should say "Dear Dad." In honor of the occasion.

AINSLEY: Thanksgiving?

ETHAN: No. Me becoming. A dad.

(Ainsley stares at him.)

ETHAN: What. *What.*

AINSLEY: I'm just . . . assimilating. Your news. "Dear Dad . . . Happy Thanksgiving."

ETHAN: Do we have his address?

AINSLEY: We have his address from . . . a few years ago. It should still work.

ETHAN: What if it doesn't?

AINSLEY: His loss. "We've had a terrific Thanksgiving."

ETHAN: What do you think they eat for Thanksgiving in Alaska?

AINSLEY: Turkey. "Lou came downstairs for the occasion. She pretty much stays in bed most of the time now. Reuben, you will remember, our tenant . . ." *(Pondering the phrasing.)* You will remember. You *will* remember, "made stuffing with roasted artichoke hearts." And now Ethan is farting them out his ears, just kidding. "You won't believe it but we finally cleared out the cake room. We need the space. Ethan's girlfriend Kimmy is going to have a baby and she's moving in. She's going to work for Mom in her video store." We should cross that out, right? A reference to Mom? *(Shrugs.)* Eh. Leave it in. "Thought you'd like to know. You're going to be a grandfather. Congratulations. Ethan and Ainsley." *(She looks at him. His eyes are tearing up.)* What's wrong? Ethan. What's wrong, sweetie?

ETHAN: I don't know. Nothing.

AINSLEY: Nothing? Your face is red, your eyes are watery.

ETHAN: I don't know. I'm happy . . . I'm . . . *(He shakes his head, throws up his arms. Grins, doesn't know what he is.)* It was . . . nice of you.

AINSLEY: What.

ETHAN: To say Kimmy should move in. That was . . . I appreciate it.

AINSLEY: Stop. Your gas is going to your head. So, were you guys using birth control at all?

ETHAN: At all?

(Ainsley just stares at him, knowing the answer.)

AINSLEY: What do you think they eat for Thanksgiving in Alaska?

ETHAN: Uh . . . I don't know if there are turkeys there. If they migrated over that . . . strait.

AINSLEY: That strait? The Bering Strait? You mean from Russia?

ETHAN: No.

(Pause.)

AINSLEY: So. Are we sending this? This is okay?

ETHAN: Should we say some more?

AINSLEY: What more?

ETHAN: I don't know.

AINSLEY: You're a mess tonight.

ETHAN: Yeah.

AINSLEY: Let's eat some pie.

ETHAN: I finished it.

AINSLEY: You finished the pie?

ETHAN: Ainsley. You're my saving grace.

AINSLEY: Is that like *Saving Private Ryan*? You finished the pie?

ETHAN: Without you . . . I don't think I'd be alive.

AINSLEY: There was half a pie left.

ETHAN: I'm sorry.

(She looks over her shoulder.)

AINSLEY: What's that noise?

ETHAN: There's a gutter loose. I'll fix it tomorrow.

(Pause.)

AINSLEY: I'm gonna start a vegetable garden this spring, back where there's all that dead brush. I'm gonna clear it out and plant a whole bunch of vegetables.

ETHAN: You want me to go to Price Chopper and buy you a pie?

AINSLEY: No.

ETHAN: I will.

AINSLEY: Price Chopper is closed.

ETHAN: We could make one.

AINSLEY: I don't know why I'm hungry.

ETHAN: Do we have the ingredients?

AINSLEY: For another pumpkin pie? Actually, we do.

ETHAN: Let's make one.

AINSLEY: Okay.

ETHAN: Let's tell Jim . . . We're making a pie. Write that. Post script. P.S.

AINSLEY: We're making a pie?

ETHAN: Yeah.

AINSLEY: All right. *(She writes.)* P.S.: We're making a pie. At midnight. In your
    mother's oven. Come on over.
ETHAN: That's nice. That's good.
    (He wipes a tear from his eye. Ainsley reaches over and grabs his hand.)
AINSLEY: Ethan, you are *my* saving grace.

THE BLUE ROOM
David Hare

Man & Woman

Scene: One of the Greatest cities in the world.

The Au Pair (eighteen) and the Student (eighteen).

Youthful hormones flare during an intimate encounter between two young people on a steamy summer day in the city.

STUDENT: What are you doing?

AU PAIR: Writing a letter.

STUDENT: I see. Who to?

AU PAIR: A man I met at a dance.

(The student does not move.)

STUDENT: It's so hot. It's so unbelievably hot. It's never this hot at this time of year. There's nobody left in town. Am I the only person still working? They didn't take you to the country?

AU PAIR: No.

(She has stopped writing but has not moved from the table.)

STUDENT: What's coolest? Vodka? Do we have vodka?

AU PAIR: We ran out. Your father drank the lot.

STUDENT: It's him who insisted I read law. It's a family tradition.

AU PAIR: The drinking?

STUDENT: The law.

(He does not acknowledge the joke.)

STUDENT: It's all right, I'll just have some water.

AU PAIR: There's the tap.

STUDENT: Can you get me a glass?

(It is clear he expects her to do it for him. She gets up, gets a glass from the cupboard, then goes to the tap, and turns it on. They are both running with sweat.)

STUDENT: Let the water run, so it's really cool.

(The water overflows from the glass into the sink. She keeps it running.)

STUDENT: Who called?

AU PAIR: I'm sorry?

STUDENT: I heard the bell ring.

AU PAIR: Did you? When?

STUDENT: Earlier.

AU PAIR: When?

STUDENT: This morning. I've been up there so long I lose all track of time. I was expecting a friend.

AU PAIR: No friend. Here.

(She has taken the glass across to him and puts it in his hand. Their hands touch.)

STUDENT: Thank you. I'll take it upstairs.

(He goes out. She goes to the mirror and adjusts her clothing, improving the line of her breasts against the shirt. She pours herself a glass of water. Before she can turn, the phone rings. She answers it.)

AU PAIR: Yes? You want another one?

(There is a slight pause.)

AU PAIR: No. You come down.

(She drinks her own glass of water. Then gets a third glass from the cupboard and pours a fresh glass. As she finishes, he appears at the door, without the book.)

STUDENT: Thank you. So, excellent. You're enjoying it here? You get on with my father?

AU PAIR: Very well.

STUDENT: My mother likes you. You relate to my mother. Which is always important, I've found.

AU PAIR: Here.

STUDENT: She's an interesting woman, don't you think?

AU PAIR: Who?

STUDENT: My mother.

(She hands him the fresh glass, and their hands touch once more.)

STUDENT: Thank you.

(He takes it, and she moves away.)

STUDENT: Do we do things differently here?

(She doesn't answer.)

STUDENT: Come here, Marie.

AU PAIR: Sir.

STUDENT: Not sir. Nobody's called sir anymore. God, I hate that idea. Those
   days are gone.

AU PAIR: Sir?

(She has moved closer to him.)

STUDENT: Please. I just wanted . . . I was looking at the shirt. Considering
   you . . . I know you have no money. Or we pay you so little, rather. And
   you have such nice things. Can I see it? Please?

(He takes the lining between finger and thumb.)

AU PAIR: What's wrong with it?

STUDENT: Nothing. It's the most beautiful blue.

AU PAIR: Sir?

STUDENT: I mean it. I'm telling the truth.

*(He puts his arm around her waist and draws her to him. She leans back as
he unbuttons her blouse a little and kisses her chest.)*

STUDENT: Your skin is beautiful. It's white.

AU PAIR: Now that's just flattery.

STUDENT: Nothing wrong with flattery, is there?

AU PAIR: No. Flattery is no harm.

(She sighs under his kisses.)

STUDENT: What a beautiful sound . . .

AU PAIR: Sir . . .

(He has suddenly dropped to her feet, still nervous.)

STUDENT: And what beautiful shoes. Blue as well. What do you call them?
   Indigo?

AU PAIR: Cobalt.

STUDENT: Are they . . . I mean, what I'm asking, do you get them from the
   same shop?

(He wraps himself around her knees.)

AU PAIR: Sir, if the doorbell rings.

STUDENT: The bell won't ring.

AU PAIR: At least close the shutters.

*(He goes across and pulls the blinds. The hot afternoon light slants through
from outside, their faces in darkness. He looks at her from across the room.)*

STUDENT: Why are you shy?

AU PAIR: You think I'm shy?

STUDENT: Anyone who looks like you has no reason to be embarrassed. If I
   looked like you, I wouldn't be shy. If I smelt like you.

(There is a pause. Neither of them move.)

STUDENT: The other evening, the bathroom door wasn't closed. You'd fallen sleep in the bath.

(They look at each other, not moving.)

AU PAIR: I'm ashamed.

STUDENT: I've seen you already. I'm halfway there, I'm already halfway there . . .

(He moves quickly across and pushes her decisively onto the butcher's block. Then he climbs on top of her. He starts to pull her skirt up, clambering over her.)

AU PAIR: What if the bell rings, what if your friend comes . . .

STUDENT: My friend won't come . . .

AU PAIR: What if he does?

STUDENT: Let him ring. Don't go to the door. Just leave him. Don't go to the door.

AU PAIR: What if he comes? What if your friend comes?

STUDENT: He won't come . . .

(Music engulfs them. Darkness. The projected slide reads: FORTY-FIVE SECONDS.)

(The music stops. The doorbell rings insistently.)

STUDENT: Oh Shit! Shit! Shit! Shit!

AU PAIR: What?

STUDENT: How long has it been ringing?

AU PAIR: It's only just started.

STUDENT: How do you know?

AU PAIR: I was listening.

(It rings again.)

STUDENT: Can you go?

AU PAIR: What?

STUDENT: Go and look through the letterbox. It may just be a beggar.

AU PAIR: You're joking.

STUDENT: I'm telling you: go and take a look.

(The Au Pair pulls down her skirt and goes out. The Student pulls up his trousers and opens the blinds. The light is liquid now, yellow. The Au Pair returns.)

AU PAIR: Whoever it was, they've gone.

STUDENT: Are you sure?

AU PAIR: Of course I'm sure.

STUDENT: Do you think it was my friend?

(He seems restless. The Au Pair doesn't notice and moves toward him again.)

AU PAIR: Well, we'll just never know.

(He looks down.)

STUDENT: I'm going to get a coffee.

AU PAIR: What?

STUDENT: I think I'd better go. I think I'd better be going. I'm going to the cafe.

(The Au Pair just looks at him.)

STUDENT: I mean it. If my friend calls . . .

AU PAIR: He won't call . . .

STUDENT: If my friend does call . . .

AU PAIR: He won't.

(There is a pause. The Student is quite angry.)

STUDENT: If he does. I am saying, Marie, if he does . . . *if* he does, please tell him where I am. Which will be in the cafe.

(He pauses a moment.)

STUDENT: I mean, if you could do your job.

AU PAIR: Sir.

(They stare at each other.)

A BORING PLAY

Christopher Mastelone

2 Men, 1 Woman

Scene: A stage.

Man, Woman and Extra (all twenties) performers on life's unchanging stage.

Here, a brainstorming session upon actors leads to an inevitable conclusion.

Note: The characters are not characters, but they are. Try figuring that one out . . .

MAN: So, what now?

WOMAN: What do you mean? We've just begun.

MAN: I know, but we have to Do something.

WOMAN: Who says? I'm happy just the way I am.

MAN: Ok. You're happy, I'm happy, but They *(The audience.)* aren't happy.

WOMAN: Shit! Forgot about them. So what should we do?

MAN: Ok . . . we do something with drama, and heart, and . . . oh yeah! Murder!

WOMAN: But if there's murder, and there are only two of us, that would turn it into a one man show. We can't do that, can we?

MAN: You're right, we have to keep two characters alive . . . I know! An extra! We bring in a person to fill that half role of the victim! It'll be great!

WOMAN: Where'll we get an extra? And why are we calling them that? This isn't a movie . . .

MAN: *(Talking over her.)* Extra!

(A person enters on the right. This is the extra:)

EXTRA: Hi!

MAN: Please sit down. Ok. Here's three people. Now we can kill the extra off at some point. *(To Extra.)* That okay with you?

EXTRA: I don't have a choice, do I?

MAN: Nope.

WOMAN: No—choice.

MAN: Condemned.

WOMAN: Finito . . .

EXTRA: Ok, I get the point . . . so what's the plot? If I'm going to die, I'm going to die for something good . . .

MAN: Ok, it goes like this. I love her, but you love her too. She loves me and we conspire against you. After tense blocks of dialogue I rush onstage, confront you, kill you, and take your wife . . . did I say she was your wife? She is now . . .

WOMAN: Nah, that sucks. Here's my idea: We are all childhood friends. We go through life together, and now we're in our thirties, and you both want me. I decide to play off your urges and make you all give me gifts, each time one-upping each other. Finally, you both give me the same gift at the same time, and a fierce fight ensues. One of you dies *(Eyes Extra.)* and one of you lives. I end up loving the dead man, and they go home happy.

EXTRA: Who?

WOMAN: What?

EXTRA: You said, "They go home happy." Who are "they"?

WOMAN: Them! *(Points to the audience.)*

EXTRA: What?

MAN: That's why you're an extra, you can't see beyond the border. Here's our world. And that's their world.

EXTRA: So wait, there are people watching us now? Whoah, all of a sudden I'm nervous, and kinda nauseous too . . .

WOMAN: That's stage fright.

MAN: You're on the stage of life, and you're in a bit role.

EXTRA: Wait a minute, that can't be good . . .

MAN: For us it's good. We get to be whatever we want, and they love us for it.

EXTRA: And what about me? I just exist to die for their fancy?

WOMAN: In a word, yes, yes you do.

EXTRA: The more I hear, the less sense this makes. Where did I come from before? No one questions that I just appeared from nowhere?

MAN: It's called "suspending your disbelief." They believe everything they see, then they talk about it later and write nasty things about us.

EXTRA: So what existed before I was here? You two were here, but what else?

WOMAN: You see, there is a mystical thing called a curtain. In most locales, it allows for creation to occur away from their prying eyes. Stars like us notice it, but you don't.

MAN: Yeah, we're around for years, but you usually appear for a few instances, then are swept away.

EXTRA: Why doth you perpetrate such crimes upon my brow?

WOMAN: What're you doing?

MAN: He's trying to steal the scene with a very poorly done Shakespeare! Quick, we've got to do something.

WOMAN: The plot! I see it now! We are existence. We have a happy little gig going, and then POW! This extra shows up. Us established stars are showing him/her the ropes when she/he has a breakout performance. Jealous of the newcomer we go ahead and kill him/her!

MAN: Brilliant!

EXTRA: Palamon, Pandar, Panthino, Puck . . . !

WOMAN: This is it! The climax of the show!

EXTRA: Montague, Macbe . . . Richard Macduff!

MAN: He's going Shakespeare! He's zoning in on a character, we just have to wait him out . . .

WOMAN: We need a knife, a club or something!

MAN: Knife! *(A knife is provided somehow.)*

EXTRA: I am . . . Sir John Falstaff from Henry the Sixth, parts one and two! This is my breakout role!

WOMAN: Now!

(Man stabs Extra, and Extra severely overacts it.)

EXTRA: I die! *(Falls down.)*

MAN: That solves that problem.

WOMAN: Damn right.

MAN: So *(Beat.)* Ever heard that quote from Brand?

WOMAN: Which one?

MAN: "Just because they say 'Action!' doesn't mean you need to do anything." I think we may have proved or disproved that right here.

WOMAN: Well this was boring. They'll want their money back. Look right there! *(Points to audience.)* That person *(Identify gender.)* is not happy! We've failed!

MAN: We have a knife? We could make this a real tragedy.

WOMAN: We are beyond respite! Woe is me!

MAN: Stop! Remember the Extra? Don't fall apart on me now. We've got to do something.

WOMAN: Run! *(Takes off, leaves the stage and general vicinity of the theater.)*

MAN: Show's over! We can't think of an ending, so we're going to be quick about it. Remember to take your personal belongings with you when you exit the theater after the show! Bye! *(He too runs.)*

(The Extra either stirs from being dead, or stands up very suddenly, to try and catch the audience thinking the scene is over. A false finish of sorts.)

EXTRA: And what now for undead extra? A noble career in stage work? Perhaps the TV? More realistically, I shall serve food to the noble lords of cinema and pitch ideas to them in the bathrooms. See you in Hollywood.

THE BRONX HEBREW SCHOOL AND SPORTS BOOK

Rooster Mitchell

Man & Woman

Scene: The Bronx Hebrew School, 1930's.

Lou (forty to fifty) President of the Bronx Hebrew School and Myrna (thirty to forty) an enigmatic old flame.

Lou is in dire need of cash to mount a proper school seder. Enter Myrna with a hot tip on a racehorse. Here, two cagey people with a smoldering past reconnect.

MYRNA: Hello, Lou.

LOU: Myrna. Been a while, huh?

MYRNA: Forever and a day, seems like.

LOU: Yes.

MYRNA: You look great.

LOU: That's *my* line.

MYRNA: All these days gone by —

LOU: . . . mm.

MYRNA: Ya know, you *could'a* picked up the phone, written a letter.

LOU: Works both ways.

MYRNA: Yes. I suppose. Girl needs to hear those words time to time, is all; I miss ya, I'm thinkin' of ya, this type a' thing.

LOU: You're here for an apology. You want me to say I'm sorry for what I done, okay, I'm —
(She interrupts him.)

MYRNA: . . . Lou. Don't. Those are mighty big words, baby, you might choke on 'em. Sides . . . *(Beats.)* It's not why I came. *(A beat.)*

LOU: Why did you come?
(A beat. Myrna looks toward the wet bar.)

MYRNA: Say. How's about a shot a' that cheap sauce for an old friend, huh?

LOU: Anything for you, doll.

(Lou walks to the wet bar, pours a glass. Myrna pulls a pack of cigarettes out of her purse, lights up.)

LOU: By the way, saw your little wink'n'nod for Jake. Goddamn adorable.

(Lou hands her the glass; she sips. Lou sits on the desk in front of Myrna.)

MYRNA: Ah gee, baby. So happens I'm fresh outta nods for you. But if you're nice, maybe I'll save you a wink on the way out.

(A beat.)

LOU: So what' this newsflash you're sittin' on?

MYRNA: He cuts to the chase —

LOU: . . . which leads to —

MYRNA: . . . business.

LOU: I'm all ears.

MYRNA: So happens I scooped up a hot tip on a fast filly comin' to town next week.

LOU: Whataya got?

MYRNA: Talked to a guy I know in Florida, owns a horse named *Angel-Eyes*, a three-year-old gem. Twelve starts, never off the board, ten wins.

LOU: Sounds like a winner.

(Myrna stands, moves about.)

MYRNA: Piece a' work, Lou. Runnin' the fifth race at the Oval next Thursday, and a smart bet would be on the ol' gal to *win*.

LOU: Is that right?

MYRNA: It's right all right.

LOU: And out of the goodness of your heart you're here with the tip.

MYRNA: This so hard to believe?

LOU: Your reputation got here ten minutes 'fore you did.

MYRNA: I'm jus' here with the news, baby.

(A beat.)

LOU: And what else?

MYRNA: How do'ya figure?

LOU: Last time you had a hot *tip*, guy dropped the whip down the backstretch.

MYRNA: Times have changed, baby. Ain't so much my policy, stingin' old chums and ex-lovers.

LOU: I might say that's a good thing.

MYRNA: Thank you.

LOU: *Then* I might say, what's it gonna set me back for the tip?

MYRNA: You've always been paranoid.

LOU: Nature of the game.

MYRNA: Well. Nature of *your* game ain't so good no more.

LOU: Myrna. Things ain't as grim as —

MYRNA: . . . Lou, who you talkin' to? A rookie? I seen the Times; they cooked your goose, baby. Wanna keep this place goin', right?

LOU: Yes.

MYRNA: Then you need dough; Haggadahs, prayer books, yarmulkes, so forth, so take charge, fight back.
  (A beat.)

LOU: So, she's a can't lose.

MYRNA: Yes.

LOU: A four legged winner.

MYRNA: That's what I'm sayin.

LOU: Who's the fella?

MYRNA: The fella?

LOU: The source, the guy?

MYRNA: An old pal down south —

LOU: . . . hm —

MYRNA: . . . guy I go back with; thought he'd do the right thing, give me the lead on the Thoroughbred.

LOU: Mm-hm.

MYRNA: Jus' a tip, baby; a tip from a friend on a can't lose.

LOU: Nothin's a can't lose, Myrn.
  (A beat, Myrna paces a bit.)

MYRNA: God-almight. You're a puzzle with a missing piece.

LOU: Ya think?

MYRNA: You trust no one.

LOU: No one that don't deserve it.

MYRNA: *I* deserve it. I deserve it *good,* all ya put me through back then.

LOU: Whataya want, Myrna? I did what seemed right —

MYRNA: . . . what seemed right was *wrong* and it tore my heart to pieces, now I'm in a jam 'cause of it, a real mess a' things.

LOU: Other words, *I* got you into something.

MYRNA: Yes . . . but you can get me out.

LOU: Mm-hmm.

MYRNA: This ain't somethin' for nothin', baby. You do right by *me* I do right by *you*, and in the end . . . who knows, maybe we both get well.

(A beat.)

LOU: What ain't ya tellin' me, Myrna?

MYRNA: Whataya sayin'?

LOU: Out of the blue, you show up, dance in with somethin' *fat*, can't wait. Sounds like a shade, half a song.

MYRNA: I need ya, Big Lou, but I won't beg'n'weep. I'm jus' here with a tip, tellin' ya what I know.

(A beat.)

MYRNA: And what I know is a filly called Angel-Eyes.

(Beat.)

When that thick wall around your heart finally tumbles down brick by brick, I *suggest* you remember that name.

(She hands the empty glass to Lou, starts to exit. She stops.)

MYRNA: . . . smart call would be puttin' your shiny nickels on her to win . . .

DINNER WITH FRIENDS
Donald Margulies
Man & Woman

Scene: A snowy night in suburban Connecticut.

Tom and Beth (forties), a couple whose marriage is definitely on the rocks.

Tom has left Beth citing a pedantic laundry list of marital complaints. Here, he returns home on the night Beth has had dinner with their best friends, complaining that it is unfair that they got to hear Beth's side of the story first. A shouting match ensues, but quickly turns into something else altogether.

BETH: Sarge! *(Pause. More barking.)* Sarge! Quiet! *(Pause. The barking persists.)* Sergeant, dammit, be quiet! *(The bedroom door opens, startling her; she gasps. Tom, in from the cold, dressed in winter gear, tracking snow in on his boots, stands there. Light from the hallway spills in.)* Tom! Jesus . . .

TOM: *(Overlap; whispers.)* Sorry. I didn't mean to . . .

BETH: *(Overlap, normal volume.)* Couldn't you at least knock?

TOM: I'm sorry.

BETH: You can't just come and go as you please anymore, Tom . . .

TOM: Shhh . . .

BETH: *(Continuous.)* . . . it's not fair; if you're gonna go, go.

TOM: I just wanted to . . .

BETH: *(Continues.)* Otherwise, I'm gonna have to change the locks.

TOM: Come on, you don't want to do *that* . . .

BETH: I *am,* that's what I'm gonna have to do.

TOM: *(Over . . . "have to do.")* Look, I didn't come here to fight. Okay? I saw the light on; I just wanted to say hi.

BETH: "Hi"?! Why aren't you in D.C.?

TOM: My flight was cancelled; they closed the airport.

BETH: Why, the snow's not that bad.

TOM: No, but it is getting worse. See? It's really starting to come down.

BETH: *(Glances out.)* Oh, shit, it is. Why didn't you get a room at the airport?

TOM: There *were* no rooms at the airport; you mean a motel?

BETH: Yeah.

TOM: There were no *rooms,* nothing, everything was booked.

BETH: Everything?

TOM: There was not a room to be had. I swear. You should've seen what was going on there. Everybody shouting and pushing . . . I just didn't have it in me to stay and sleep on the floor.

BETH: Why didn't you call your friend, the stewardess?

TOM: *(Wearily.)* Travel agent.

BETH: Whatever.

TOM: I did.

BETH: And? Couldn't *she* help you? With all her many connections?

TOM: Not really; no. I was forty-five minutes from home. All I could think about . . . was coming home. *(They share eye contact. Off her look:)* Don't worry, I'm sleeping in the den.

BETH: Who's worried?

TOM: Well, look, I just wanted to say hi.

BETH: You're melting.

TOM: Huh?

BETH: Your boots. You're making a puddle.

TOM: Oh. Sorry . . . *(He sits to remove his boots.)* I looked in on the kids; they both look pretty wrecked.

BETH: Oh, yeah, they partied hearty. Sam fell asleep in the car. I made a successful transfer, though; he didn't budge.

TOM: He's snoring his head off in there.

BETH: He's getting a cold.

TOM: *(Sympathetically.)* Oh no . . .

BETH: His nose was runny all night. I gave him some Tylenol before we left Karen and Gabe's.

TOM: Liquid or chewable?

BETH: Liquid.

TOM: Wow. And he let you? He usually puts up such a fight. Remember how he'd make himself gag?

BETH: *(Discomfited by the familiarity of their conversation, she changes the subject.)* Yeah, well, look, I'd really like to be alone right now if you don't mind . . .

TOM: *(Over ". . . if you don't mind . . .")* Yeah, sure . . .

BETH: Your bedding's in the dryer.

TOM: Oh. Thanks.

BETH: I threw everything in the wash. I wasn't expecting you back.

TOM: I know. Thank you. I'll . . .

BETH: You might want to grab an extra blanket while you're at it; sounds like it might get pretty cold in there tonight.

TOM: Good idea, thanks. *(Gets blanket from a chest. Sees the place mats.)* What's this?

BETH: Oh. For us. From Italy. A little house gift. Very homey, no? Karen and Gabe, God love 'em, they know what a disaster I am in the kitchen so they're always giving me things like trivets and cookbooks.

TOM: *(Smiles, then:)* How was dinner?

BETH: Fabulous. *You* know. When is dinner there *not* fabulous?

TOM: What was it this time?

BETH: Oh, *you* know. These incredible recipes they picked up in Italy. Pumpkin risotto, grilled lamb . . .

TOM: Mm. That *does* sound good. You didn't bring any home by any chance?

BETH: No; I did not.

TOM: The kids eat that, too?

BETH: Of course not, what do you think? They would never eat anything that good. No, Gabe cooked up some macaroni and cheese for them. From scratch. That was almost as good as the risotto.

TOM: *(A beat.)* So how are they?

BETH: They're fine. *You* know. As always. They went on and on about Italy. Thank God their slides weren't back yet.

TOM: *(Smiles, then:)* So what did you tell them?

BETH: About what?

TOM: Why I wasn't there.

BETH: I said you had to go to D.C.

TOM: And they accepted that?

BETH: Why shouldn't they accept that? You're always going *some*where . . .

TOM: Yeah, but they didn't suspect anything?

BETH: No.

TOM: What did they say?

BETH: What do you mean, what did they say? What did they say about what?

TOM: About my not being there.

BETH: They said they were sorry.

TOM: Sorry about what?

BETH: About your not being there! Jesus! Are you gonna cross-*examine* me now? Look, I'm tired, I'm going to sleep . . .

TOM: I just want to get an idea of what you all talked about, that's all.

BETH: I told you. Italy and stuff. They talked about this famous old Italian cook they're doing a piece on.

TOM: And?

BETH: I don't know, Tom, we talked about a lot of things; what do we ever talk about?

TOM: I don't know, what *do* we talk about?

BETH: Movies, kids, money, the news. I don't know, what we saw, what we read. Karen's mom has cataracts; she has to have surgery.

TOM: Is that it?

BETH: I don't know, I don't remember every single goddamn thing.

TOM: You were there like five or six hours.

BETH: Oh, please . . .

TOM: Right? Like from five to ten, ten-thirty?

BETH: So?

TOM: That's a lot of hours to fill with talk. You mean to tell me the whole evening went by without a word about us?

BETH: You are so paranoid, you know that?

TOM: Oh, really, am I?

BETH: *(Gets under the covers, turns away.)* Look, I'm really not in the mood for this . . .

TOM: You told them.

BETH: What?!

TOM: You did! You told them!

BETH: Oh, God . . .

TOM: I can tell by looking at you! I *knew* I shouldn't've trusted you!

BETH: Shhh! You want to wake up the whole house?!

TOM: *(Continuous.)* We were gonna get a sitter and tell them together, face to face, remember?! That's all I asked. Wait for me to get back, we'll tell them together.

BETH: *(Over ". . . we'll tell them together.")* If it was really so important to you, you should've just come tonight, instead of running off to be with your girlfriend!

TOM: Shit, where were the kids?

BETH: What?

TOM: Where were the kids when you told them?

BETH: I don't know . . .

TOM: You don't *know?!* Were they *sitting* there?!

BETH: No, of course not. They were upstairs, I guess, watching a tape.

TOM: What were they watching?

BETH: What?!

TOM: What tape were they watching?

BETH: Christ, I don't know, Tom . . .

TOM: You don't know what tape your own children were watching?!

BETH: Oh, for God's sake . . . I don't know, some Disney thing. *The Aristocats.*

TOM: *(Pacing, agitated.)* So, the kids are upstairs watching *The Aristocats* and you're where?

BETH: This is ridiculous.

TOM: No no, I want to get the whole picture. The kids are upstairs and you're in the living room? Huh?

BETH: *(Reluctantly.)* At the table.

TOM: Middle of dinner?

BETH: Right before dessert.

TOM: What was it?

BETH: What.

TOM: The dessert.

BETH: Some kind of lemon-almond cake, made with polenta.

TOM: Was it great?

BETH: Yes.

TOM: So you're sitting there . . .

BETH: I don't believe this.

TOM: Tell me.

BETH: We were sitting there . . . and I lost it. I just . . . lost it.

TOM: Oh, Christ . . . You *cried?* You actually *cried?*

BETH: Yes. What do you expect? Of course I cried.

TOM: Shit!

BETH: *You* try carrying that around with you. I'm only human. I mean, I'm sitting there with our closest friends . . .

TOM: I can't believe you did this . . .

BETH: *(Continuous.)* . . . eating their food, drinking their wine, making believe that everything is just dandy, and I couldn't do it!

TOM: I can't believe it . . .

BETH: So what? So what if they know? So they know! They were bound to find out!

TOM: That's not the point! *You've* got the advantage now!

BETH: What?! I do not!

TOM: Of course you do! You got to them first!

BETH: Tom . . .

TOM: *(Continuous.)* They heard your side of the story first! Of *course* they're gonna side with you, it's only natural!

BETH: Oh, come on, nobody's taking sides.

TOM: Don't be naive! You know how it is! I'm not gonna let you get away with this . . .

BETH: What?!

TOM: *(Continuous.)* Gabe and Karen mean too much to me, I'm not gonna let you turn them against me!

BETH: Tom, you're overreacting.

TOM: Don't tell me I'm overreacting! You've prejudiced my case!

BETH: I have not, Tommy. I was very evenhanded.

TOM: How can you say that?! You're sitting there turning on the tears . . .

BETH: I wasn't turning on anything! Fuck you; I stated the facts. They were very sympathetic.

TOM: Of course they were sympathetic. You won them over.

BETH: I did not; stop saying that.

TOM: You *intended* to tell them.

BETH: That is not true! I tried, I really did. I couldn't help it! Everything just spilled out!

TOM: Tell me. What did you spill? I want to hear what you spilled.

BETH: Look, this is sick. I'm exhausted. Aren't you exhausted, Tom?

TOM: *(Over "Aren't you exhausted, Tom?")* I want to know what was said. Do you mind? I'm entitled to know.

BETH: You *know* all this, we've been through this a dozen times.

TOM: *(Over ". . . a dozen times.")* If you're gonna be speaking for the both of us, the least you could do . . .

BETH: I told them what happened. Okay?

TOM: Everything?

BETH: *(A beat.)* Yes.

TOM: And what did they say?

BETH: They were shocked. They were sad.

TOM: They were?

BETH: What do you think? They're our best friends. Of course, they were shocked, they were terribly upset.

TOM: They were sad for *you*, though, right? Because *I'm* such a bastard.

BETH: They were sad for everybody. They were sad for the kids.

TOM: Did you tell them what you did to me, how you killed my self-confidence?

BETH: Oh, Christ, Tom . . .

TOM: *(Continuous.)* Did you? Did you tell them how you refused to hear me? How I tried to get you to listen to me — for years — but you wouldn't? Did you tell them that?

BETH: *(Over "Did you tell them that?")* No more of this. Please?

TOM: I cried out for help, so many times . . .

BETH: How did you cry out, Tom, by fucking stewardesses?

TOM: Goddammit, she's not a stewardess!

BETH: Were your cries detectable by *human* ears, Tom, or could just the *dogs* in the neighborhood hear them?

TOM: That's right, go ahead, cut me down, castrate me all over again.

BETH: *(Over ". . . all over again.")* Oh, please. You know, I hear you say this stuff, Tom . . . I can't believe that someone I could have been married to, for *twelve years!*, that I could have had *children* with!, would be capable of spouting such banal bullshit!

TOM: Even now! Even now you're doing it! Even now you refuse to hear me!

BETH: I "hear" you, I "hear" you! Christ! Tell me your *girl*friend feeds you this crap, Tommy, I can't believe you came up with it on your own!

TOM: Don't patronize me; I don't need *Nancy* to tell me what I'm feeling . . .

BETH: *(Over "I don't need Nancy to . . .")* Don't talk to me about being patronized! You patronized *me,* all along! From the very beginning!

TOM: I patronized *you?*

BETH: Yes! Admit it, you never took me seriously as an artist! Never!

TOM: *(Over "Never!")* Oh, for God's sake . . .

BETH: You didn't! You never really supported me!

TOM: I supported you! I supported you our entire marriage, how can you say I didn't support you?! You got a great deal! You needed more time to yourself? Help with the kids? I got you a nanny . . .

BETH: *Me* a nanny?

TOM: *(Continuous.)* You needed your own space? I built you one over the garage! God only knows what the hell you *do* up there all day.

BETH: All I ever wanted from you was *respect,* you know that? For me, for my art . . .

TOM: Ah, your art, your art.

BETH: What's the use? Get out of here. Go. Get out.

TOM: *(Over "Go . . .")* You held this marriage *hostage* to your goddamn art!

BETH: Out!

TOM: Do you know what it's like having to support something you don't believe in? Do you, Beth? It's exhausting.

BETH: *(Turning away.)* I don't want to talk anymore . . .

TOM: The lying, lying to you, lying to myself . . .

BETH: Go away! Get out!

TOM: *(Over "Get out!")* What was I supposed to tell you, that I thought your "art" sucked?

BETH: Bastard . . .

TOM: *(Continuous.)* Huh? Is that what I was supposed to say? That it was just an excuse not to get a fucking job like everybody else . . .

BETH: You are such a fucking bastard.

TOM: *(Continuous.)* . . . and really *do* something with your life?!

BETH: How dare you! How *dare* you!

TOM: *(Continuous.)* I couldn't do that; how could I? Everything depended on perpetuating this myth of talent! *(She strikes him. He grabs her wrists.)* You wanna fight? Huh? You wanna hit me? *(He gets into the bed, straddles her.)*

BETH: *(Overlap.)* Let go of me! Let *go* of me!

TOM: *(Overlap.)* Hit me! Hit me! Go ahead and hit me!

BETH: Prick!

TOM: Bitch! *(She spits in his face. They wrestle, roll around on the bed, inflaming their conflicted passions.)* Ballbreaker!

BETH: Liar!

TOM: Dilettante!

BETH: You fuck!

TOM: Look at me! Look what you've done to me!

BETH: Look what you've done to *me!*

TOM: I could kill you! Right now, I could fucking kill you!

BETH: Try it. I dare you. *(They're looking at one another. He suddenly kisses her hard on the mouth. Pause. Equally aroused, she quickly undoes his pants as lights fade.)*

GOING TO BORDEAUX
Richard Lay
Man & Woman

Scene: A small town in Maine.

Nell (forties), an unhappy wife, and Vincent (forties), her unfaithful husband.

Nell and Vincent's relationship is teetering on the edge of disaster, as the following confrontation reveals.

Nell sitting on a sofa reading a newspaper. Enter Vincent. Nell looks up.

NELL: *(Flat voice.)* Hello . . . had a good day?

VINCENT: *(Pause.)* No.

NELL: Where have you been?

VINCENT: Nowhere special . . . Checking on things,

NELL: What things?

VINCENT: Nothing you . . .

NELL: . . . need to worry my little head about.

VINCENT: Don't start.

NELL: Start what?

VINCENT: You know what I mean.

NELL: Start what?

VINCENT: Start on me.

NELL: I've heard it before.

VINCENT: And you've never listened Nell.

NELL: You were supposed to do it a year ago.

VINCENT: *(Agitated.)* I've started planning. Checking on things . . . I'm moving out. I'm living somewhere else for six months of the year.

NELL: Why not make it twelve months a year?

VINCENT: Don't . . . Please don't . . . You know it's been tough.

NELL: No it hasn't. *(Sarcastic.)* It's been lovely. I've never been happier. So the sooner it happens . . . the better.

VINCENT: I hate this place . . . I loved New York, I loved painting in Greenwich Village . . .But, oh no, you hate what I love . . . and here we are in a Maine fishing village . . . If I have another fucking lobster dinner I'll throw up.

NELL: Vincent, we've been together a long time . . . our kids are grown up *(Pause.)* . . . We never married . . . as I tell our friends.

VINCENT: What friends?

NELL: The bums who come up from New York and sketch in the backyard and eat our food and drink our wine . . . I tell them "Vincent and I are OK . . . we're not in love. But we LOVE each other."

VINCENT: *(Indignant.)* And where'd you get that cliché . . . one of the cheap novels you feed your head with at the same time as you are stuffing yourself with chocolates.

NELL: *(Pause.)* You used to be a charming man.

VINCENT: Who could be charming living with you?

NELL: You once said you'd die for me.

VINCENT: I must have been depressed.

NELL: You once said you'd jump off the Washington Square arch if I asked you.

VINCENT: That sort of proves my point.

NELL: No Vincent, I know you did love me once.

VINCENT: How?

NELL: Remember when I was twenty-five and you sent that singing telegram and my Dad answered the door and this guy dressed up as a moose sang "You're driving me crazy."

VINCENT: I don't know what you're talking about.

NELL: Yes you do.

VINCENT: I'm going you know.

NELL: *(Airily sarcastic.)* Oh yes, going to Bordeaux to paint pictures. France, and all that natural light, nude models lining up at your door . . . a patron here, a patron there. Endless wine in your declining years. Up at dawn — I don't think — to pursue your precious art.

VINCENT: Is it too much to ask to be free six months of the year?

NELL: That means I can do what I want. Pursue my interests.

VINCENT: *(Laughs.)* What interests?

NELL: You don't know everything.

VINCENT: All I know — is that you sleep in the bedroom in a double bed and

I sleep on the narrow canvas bed in my studio . . . with paint fumes invading my lungs.

NELL: You could always stop painting.

VINCENT: You could always stop breathing.

(Phone rings. Nell picks it up.)

NELL: Hello, darling. Fine . . . fine . . . No you didn't interrupt dinner. Your father and I were just having a quiet evening *(She looks at Vincent.)* . . . just looking at the photo albums . . . No, no, I won't. I knew it was coming up but you didn't know when . . . No, I won't. OK darling . . . Do you want to talk to your father . . . No, OK, I'll tell him. Byee *(She puts phone down.)* . . . That was Dana . . . She had to run . . . Sent her love.

VINCENT: What's wrong?

NELL: Nothing.

VINCENT: You're lying.

NELL: There's nothing wrong.

VINCENT: *(Menacing.)* What did you mean when you said to her "No, No, I won't"?

NELL: Won't what?

VINCENT: You're trying to deceive me. You know you said "No, no, I won't."

NELL: In what context?

VINCENT: Goddammit . . . you said it *(Raises hands, outstretched and lowers them slowly.)* . . . Very clever . . . Trying to get my blood pressure up. *(Gruff.)* Is that it?

NELL: *(Calmly, sweet smile.)* Why would I want to do that, Vincent?

VINCENT: To spite me.

NELL: *(Shaking her head slowly.)* Why would I want to spite you?

VINCENT: Because I know how to be free.

NELL: *(Cynical.)* Oh yes, that's what you said isn't it — in that calm voice that is supposed to explain all your inner thoughts. Nell, you said, I just want to spend six months of the year in Bordeaux . . . slapping paint on canvas. Let me explain . . . that phone call we just had and when I said "No, no, I won't" — it was obvious wasn't it . . . She, our lovely daughter, told me something she didn't want YOU to know about.

VINCENT: She'd never do that.

NELL: She just did.

VINCENT: What's her number?

NELL: You should know.

VINCENT: *(Almost pleading.)* You know I never write anything down.

NELL: *(Smiling.)* Tough.

VINCENT: *(Tense/patient.)* What's her number?

NELL: *(Triumphant smile.)* I'd throw you the phone book — but she's not listed.

VINCENT: *(Angry.)* What's her fucking number?

NELL: The truth is Vincent, darling husband who wants to go to Bordeaux, is that she gave it to you for your birthday as a present for letting her live in her own apartment . . . *(Smirk.)* I think you threw it away one night when you were drunk and cleared out your desk on a whim.

VINCENT: And you let me?

NELL: You didn't ask me not to.

VINCENT: You let me. You saw what I was doing.

NELL: *(Airily.)* I thought you knew what you were doing.

VINCENT: I never let you know what I'm doing.

NELL: Oh my, do I detect honesty. You never let me know what you are doing . . . you have proved that time and time again. Open book Vincent, you always have been.

VINCENT: *(Slowly.)* I hate to say for the last time but . . . are you going to tell me what my daughter, our daughter Dana meant.

NELL: I might.

VINCENT: You might it what?

NELL: If you tell me what you are really up to . . . you see I know she is behind it.

VINCENT: She?

NELL: Your prize art student Charley . . . Your prize fuck . . . Your prize lover.

VINCENT: *(Sits down and then stands up and smiles.)* Charley happens to be a brilliant artist. *(Walks toward Nell.)* She attached herself to me because she's a very insecure kid. No, no, no . . . we have never slept together . . . my decision to go to Bordeaux has nothing to do with her. *(Opens hands.)* She lives in Brooklyn with her folks and works in their deli and does flower bouquets for weddings . . . A nice girl.

NELL: You talk about her in your sleep.

VINCENT: How would you know? You're too busy talking in your own sleep.

NELL: You scream her name, not just say it. You say her name and scream.

VINCENT: *(Slowly.)* It's a thick wall between your bedroom and my studio.

NELL: It's a thin door.

VINCENT: *(Earnest.)* What's wrong with Dana?

NELL: She's pregnant . . . That's all. Nothing to worry about. She just doesn't want YOU to know yet.

VINCENT: Abortion?

NELL: No.

VINCENT: She's eighteen.

NELL: She wants it.

VINCENT: Whose is it?

NELL: She won't say . . . *(Smiles.)* Grandad.

VINCENT: *(Angry.)* Don't you call me that.

NELL: Anyway, the plan was that I told you when you were calm.

VINCENT: I'm not a grandad until it's born.

NELL: In about seven months.

VINCENT: Where's it gonna live?

NELL: Where do you think?

VINCENT: What does the father say?

NELL: He doesn't know.

VINCENT: How do you know that when you say "She won't say who he is."

NELL: There's a bit more to it than meets the eye. OK Vincent, you despicable bastard — I will call our lovely daughter and you can talk to her as long as you promise not to upset her. I could never understand that now we live in the country with pigs and sheep and chickens that you always shout "Charley" when the cocks crow at first light with their chorus of . . . another sun, another day, more eggs to be hatched, a broken neck here and there if it was their turn for the pot. Funny that, isn't it?

Charley on your lips even before your brain wakes up.

HUMAN EVENTS
A.R. Gurney
Man & Woman

Scene: Here and now.

Porter and Nancy (both forties), a couple whose marriage is in a bit of trouble.

Here, Nancy makes several confessions which definitely rock Porter's world.

Nancy enters on tip-toe, in her overcoat, carrying her tote bag. She quietly takes off her coat and hangs it up. Porter comes on, in a sweater.

PORTER: *(Kissing her.)* I was worried.
NANCY: I had a test.
PORTER: How did it go?
NANCY: I flunked.
PORTER: You always say that, and then pass with flying colors.
NANCY: This time I know.
PORTER: They've already graded it?
NANCY: I graded myself.
PORTER: You had a new kind of test tonight?
NANCY: I had an affair tonight.
    (Pause.)
PORTER: With your Nigerian gentleman?
NANCY: Yes.
PORTER: Why?
NANCY: Why? I don't know why. Maybe because things have been so rocky lately between you and me.
PORTER: Can't deny that.
NANCY: There he was, this young, attractive, sexy man, always turning around to smile at me in class, always asking me out for coffee afterwards.
PORTER: Working with you on the pumpkin project.
NANCY: All that. And tonight, after the coffee, he asked me to his apartment.

He said his roommates weren't there. So I thought about it. And said Yes.

PORTER: That was the test?

NANCY: That was the test.

PORTER: How did you flunk?

NANCY: He put these African tunes on the stereo, which I didn't know how to dance to, and we smoked some pot, which just made me more self-conscious, and finally one of his roommates came back, and I grabbed my stuff and ran.

PORTER: So nothing happened.

NANCY: No. *(Pause.)* I mean, yes.

PORTER: You went to bed with him?

NANCY: It didn't mean anything, Porter. I felt terrible the whole time — cheap and guilty and old.

PORTER: That's how you flunked?

NANCY: That's how I flunked.

PORTER: Hmmm.

(Thinks; then magnanimously.)

You passed, Nancy. In my book, you passed.

NANCY: You think?

PORTER: I do. And I admit I've been a lousy husband lately.

NANCY: We've both been bad.

PORTER: I've been worse. I want to tell you about what happened between me and Anita.

NANCY: *(Interrupting.)* It happened with Chris, too, you know.

PORTER: I wanted to teach in Anita's writing course, so I —

NANCY: *(Interrupting again.)* I said it happened with Chris.

PORTER: *(Exploding.)* WHAT?

NANCY: Here we go.

PORTER: What the fuck did you do with Chris?

NANCY: Calm down.

PORTER: In this house?

NANCY: Sssh. the kids.

PORTER: In my home?

NANCY: Yes!

PORTER: When, goddammit, when?

NANCY: Last fall. When he stayed with us after his trip west.

PORTER: *(Walking away.)* I don't want to know

NANCY: O.K., you don't have to.

PORTER: *(Wheeling on her.)* TELL me!

NANCY: It was a Saturday afternoon . . .

PORTER: Where were the kids?

NANCY: Out, obviously . . . So was the dog.

PORTER: I don't give a shit about the dog.

NANCY: That's something new.

PORTER: Go ON, goddammit!

NANCY: You and I had just had another fight, so you'd run off to the Red Sox game, and I thought I'd take a bath and listen to *The Marriage of Figaro*.

PORTER: Where was Chris?

NANCY: I'm trying to *tell* you, Porter . . . So after our fight, I put on the stereo, and got in the tub, and was listening to that sad aria by the Countess when she feels so alone. "Dove sono i bei momenti" . . . Where are the beautiful moments?

PORTER: I don't give a shit about the beautiful moments.

NANCY: Well I do!

PORTER: Go on, go on.

NANCY: There was a knock on the bathroom door.

PORTER: Chris?

NANCY: He had made me a cup of tea.

PORTER: Goddam British and their fucking tea!

NANCY: If you're going to start stereotyping people again, I won't say another word.

PORTER: No, go on. He brought you tea. What did you say?

NANCY: I said thank you, and please leave it outside the door.

PORTER: And he said?

NANCY: He asked if he could bring it in.

PORTER: WHAT?

NANCY: He said he had always admired my body and wanted to see me naked.

PORTER: And you said?

NANCY: I said O.K.!

PORTER: Jesus, Nancy!

NANCY: Yes well remember, Porter. Not too many people have made that request recently.

PORTER: O.K. I hear you. Go on.

NANCY: So he came into the bathroom and handed me the tea.

PORTER: And that's all?

NANCY: No. He asked if he could get into the tub with me.

PORTER: That CREEP!

NANCY: The English like to take baths, Porter!

PORTER: Bastard!

NANCY: You've done it too, Porter. Remember when the Danforths went skinny dipping? You joined right in!

PORTER: All right, all right. Go on.

NANCY: So he took off his clothes and got in. But the tub was too small. American tubs aren't as big as British tubs, Porter. The water was spilling all over the bathroom floor. We could have had a serious leak!

PORTER: Oh really.

NANCY: So we jumped out, and put on our clothes, and toweled up the mess, and then drank tea and listened to the rest of the opera downstairs. And when it was finished we shook hands and he left.

PORTER: That's all?

NANCY: That's all.

PORTER: The guy probably couldn't make it with you anyway.

NANCY: Not true. Not true at all.

PORTER: How do you know?

NANCY: You could tell.

PORTER: The bastard.

NANCY: We even discussed it. He said it wouldn't be cricket.

PORTER: "Wouldn't be cricket?" To who? Barbara Birdfeather?

NANCY: To you, ya jerk! And I agreed.

PORTER: This is a bad dream!

NANCY: No, sweetheart, listen. with my Nigerian friend, things happened and it meant nothing. With Chris, nothing happened and it meant everything!

PORTER: Why everything?

NANCY: Because it was all about you . . . But you know something? I am suddenly terribly, terribly tired. Do you mind if I go to bed?

PORTER: How could you possibly sleep?

NANCY: Because I've finally gotten this off my chest. Coming up?

PORTER: No.

NANCY: Please.

PORTER: I have to think things out.

NANCY: So should I. I should think about . . . who'd you say it was? Anita?

PORTER: It didn't amount to —

NANCY: I know . . . But won't it be nice when we don't have to talk about who we've been fooling around with?

PORTER: Nancy . . .

NANCY: Good night, sweetie. I think we're both the better for this. In the long run. Thanks to Chris.

(She goes.)

LAST TRAIN TO NIBROC
Arlene Hutton
Man & Woman

Scene: A cross-country train, December 1940.

May (twenties), from a small town in Kentucky, sincere and honest in her beliefs, and Raleigh (twenties), from a nearby town, just a good guy, slow to anger and quick to chuckle.

Here, bookish May encounters Raleigh, a flyer who has just received a medical discharge. These two seemingly opposites quickly find that they have much more in common than they may have thought.

RALEIGH: Mind if I . . . *(May keeps reading her book.)* Mind if I set a spell?
    (Raleigh gestures to the empty seat beside her.)
MAY: *(After a beat.)* Don't make no nevermind to me.
    (May keeps reading her book. A pause.)
RALEIGH: This train —
MAY: Yes?
RALEIGH: This train's very —
MAY: Yes, it's —
RALEIGH: Full. Crowded.
MAY: Yes.
RALEIGH: *(Smiling at her.)* I was lucky to get a seat.
MAY: Yes. *(Looking around.)* But —
RALEIGH: Do you mind me sitting here?
MAY: I don't know you.
RALEIGH: I was standing all night.
MAY: Standing?
RALEIGH: Until the train stopped at this station.
MAY: Yes, it was full —
RALEIGH: It was packed leaving California. I got on in Los Angeleese. *(Pause.)*
    What'ya reading?
MAY: Pardon?

RALEIGH: Your book.

MAY: Oh. *(May looks at the cover of the book.)* It's *Magnificent Obsession.*

RALEIGH: *(Gently teasing.)* Sounds pretty racy.

MAY: *(Taking him seriously.)* No. Not at all.

RALEIGH: A romance.

MAY: It's more religious . . .

RALEIGH: *(Still teasing.)* There's no romance in it?

MAY: It's not about that.

RALEIGH: There's not a girl and a guy?

MAY: Well, there is, but —

RALEIGH: It must be a love story.

MAY: It's not. I don't read —

RALEIGH: It's a love story. Has to be.

MAY: *(Flustered.)* Why?

RALEIGH: With a title like that. *Magnificent Obsession.*

MAY: That's not what the title is about.

RALEIGH: Not what?

MAY: Not about.

RALEIGH: Not about what?

MAY: Romance. A love story. What you — It's not about —
   (She pauses.)

RALEIGH: *(Simply.)* What is it about? Your book. What's it about?

MAY: This man — *(She stops.)*

RALEIGH: Do they kiss?

MAY: What?

RALEIGH: In the book?

MAY: *(Simply.)* I haven't finished it yet.

RALEIGH: Oh.

MAY: But it's religious.

RALEIGH: Uh-huh.

MAY: It is. It's from the church library. The library at church. It's religious.
   (May goes back to her book. A pause.)

RALEIGH: Are you?

MAY: What?

RALEIGH: Religious?

MAY: Well, yes.

RALEIGH: *(Pause.)* It's about a doctor. *(Pause.)* Your book.

MAY: You've read it!

RALEIGH: A couple years ago. I read everything.

MAY: Don't tell me the ending.

RALEIGH: It's a romance.

MAY: No, it's —

RALEIGH: Religious?

MAY: Well, inspirational.

(A pause.)

RALEIGH: You like to read?

MAY: Well, yes.

RALEIGH: I like to write.

MAY: *(Interested.)* Really? You're a writer?

RALEIGH: Gonna be. *(Pause.)* There's writers on this train.

MAY: How do you know?

RALEIGH: Porter over yonder told me. He let me sit in the men's room for a while.

MAY: I thought you didn't have a seat.

RALEIGH: That's good.

MAY: What is?

RALEIGH: That's funny.

MAY: It's not funny that you had to sit in the —

RALEIGH: I thought it was lucky. Like having a private room.

MAY: A private room with running water.

RALEIGH: With hot and cold running water.

MAY: *(Laughs.)* You're funny.

RALEIGH: So're you. *(They smile at each other. A pause. May picks up her book again.)* The porter told me there's writers on the train.

MAY: Riders? People riding the train?

RALEIGH: Writers. Authors.

MAY: Well, there's lots of people on the train.

RALEIGH: Guess who's riding this train with us.

MAY: I don't like to guess.

RALEIGH: No, just guess. You can't.

MAY: I know I can't guess, so I won't even try.

RALEIGH: Two of them.

MAY: Two what?

RALEIGH: Authors. Famous ones.

MAY: Who?

RALEIGH: Guess!

MAY: I don't — *(May reads from the spine of her book.)* Lloyd C. Douglas?

RALEIGH: Nope.

MAY: William Shakespeare?

RALEIGH: You're not even trying.

MAY: I don't care.

RALEIGH: Very famous writers.

MAY: Who, then?

RALEIGH: Nathanael West!

MAY: Who's that?

RALEIGH: You don't know who Nathanael West is?

MAY: No.

RALEIGH: He's a great novelist. *The Day of the Locust. Miss Lonelyhearts.*

MAY: I don't read books like that.

RALEIGH: Books like what?

MAY: Lonely heart books. Romances.

RALEIGH: They're not — What do you read? Besides . . . *(Raleigh indicates her book.)*

MAY: Inspirational stories.

RALEIGH: F. Scott Fitzgerald.

MAY: No.

RALEIGH: He inspired me.

MAY: That's not what I meant.

RALEIGH: He's on this train, too.

MAY: Is not.

RALEIGH: Is so. F. Scott Fitzgerald is riding on this train. Going to New York City.

MAY: You're making it up.

RALEIGH: Do you even know who he is?

MAY: Of course.

RALEIGH: Have you read his books?

MAY: No.

RALEIGH: Well, he's on this train. F. Scott Fitzgerald.

MAY: But he's dead, silly. He died. He died a few days ago. I read about it in the newspaper.

RALEIGH: He's on the train.

MAY: He's dead.

RALEIGH: He's in the baggage car.

(A pause.)

MAY: You're crazy.

RALEIGH: His coffin.

MAY: Pardon?

RALEIGH: His coffin is riding in the baggage car. F. Scott Fitzgerald is on this train. He's riding the same train we are.

MAY: Oh. *(Pause.)* How do you know?

RALEIGH: Porter told me.

MAY: Oh.

RALEIGH: With Nathanael West.

MAY: He's with him?

RALEIGH: His coffin, too. We're riding with two of the greatest authors of the century. We're all on this train together.

MAY: That's morbid.

RALEIGH: It's funny, what puts people on trains together.

MAY: Mmmm. *(May looks out the window.)* Where are we?

RALEIGH: Don't know. *(Raleigh tries to look out her window.)* Can't tell. But the sun's about to come up.

MAY: It's black as pitch.

RALEIGH: Little light over yonder. See? Just a glimpse of the sunrise.

(He leans over her even more to see out.)

MAY: You can't have this seat.

RALEIGH: *(Surprised.)* I don't want it.

MAY: Well, you can't have it!

RALEIGH: I never said —

MAY: You just want the window seat so you can sleep. Lean your head against the window.

RALEIGH: No, it's yours.

MAY: You're right. It's mine. And I'm not giving it up.

RALEIGH: Look, miss.

MAY: *(Starting to cry.)* I came all the way out here sitting on the aisle seat. People bumping me and I never got to sleep at all and I couldn't look out the window most of the time and there were small children running around. I like children —

RALEIGH: — of course you do —

MAY: — but not when they're running up and down the aisles a' screaming. And bumping my arm so I couldn't sleep for the life of me, not even doze, and there was this man —

RALEIGH: — a man?

MAY: — for hours, just hours, in the window seat here, and I couldn't find another seat, and I had to sit up straight and he —

RALEIGH: — what?

MAY: *(Really crying now.)* — he smelled. He just smelled bad. And the train and the smell made me sick and I had to — well, I almost had to, well, be sick.

RALEIGH: Oh, that's too bad.

MAY: But I wasn't. And so I'm not giving up this seat to anyone, not my window seat, not to anyone, especially not to a soldier!
(A pause.)

RALEIGH: Would you like my handkerchief?

MAY: I have my own, thank you very much.

RALEIGH: May I get it for you? Your handkerchief.

MAY: *(Sobbing.)* It's in my suitcase. *(She looks up towards the overhead shelf.)*

RALEIGH: Here's mine, then. Take it. You need a handkerchief.

MAY: I'm just so tired. I don't know what to do.

RALEIGH: *(At a loss.)* Uh-huh.

MAY: It's been so awful.

RALEIGH: It will get better.

MAY: I don't see how. *(Pause.)* I have to go home.

RALEIGH: Well, that's good, isn't it?

MAY: I don't know how I can face them. My family.

RALEIGH: Please don't mind my asking this.

MAY: You're being very nice. And you don't even know me.

RALEIGH: You're afraid to go home to your family.

MAY: Not afraid. Ashamed.

RALEIGH: Is there? . . . Are you? . . . You felt ill.

MAY: No.

RALEIGH: On the trip out. You said . . .

MAY: You think I'm . . . delicate?

RALEIGH: You said that you —

MAY: Oh, no. I'd never. How can you think that of me?

RALEIGH: I don't.

MAY: They'll think that.

RALEIGH: Your family.

MAY: They'll think that we . . . that I.

(May starts to sob again.)

RALEIGH: But you're not.

MAY: Of course not!

RALEIGH: Well, that's good then.

MAY: We were engaged.

RALEIGH: A soldier.

MAY: Well, he's training. To fly. Yes.

RALEIGH: You went out to see him. Before he went to England.

MAY: Yes. For Christmas.

RALEIGH: That was a nice thing for you to do.

MAY: No. He was different. He's changed.

(A pause.)

RALEIGH: And now you're going home.

MAY: Yes.

RALEIGH: Home, where? Where's home?

MAY: Kentucky. Corbin. Corbin, Kentucky.

RALEIGH: No.

MAY: Yes. Corbin.

RALEIGH: I'm from Woodbine, Kentucky.

MAY: You're not.

RALEIGH: Yes, I am.

MAY: Well, how about that.

RALEIGH: How about that. Just a few miles apart.

MAY: So you're going to Woodbine?

RALEIGH: No, I'm just from there. I'm going to New York City.

MAY: You're not changing trains?

RALEIGH: No, I was. In the beginning. Almost. But I want to go to New York City.

MAY: You out of the service?

RALEIGH: Um, well, yeah.

MAY: Aren't you itching to go? Go overseas?

RALEIGH: I was.

MAY: Most people volunteering. Going into the service. I don't know anybody leaving the service.

RALEIGH: Medical. *(A pause.)*

MAY: I'm sorry. *(An awkward pause.)*

RALEIGH: It was hard to leave my buddies.

MAY: I would imagine it was. But don't you want to see your family?

RALEIGH: They'll be ashamed I'm not off flying like I said I was gonna do.

MAY: They'd be glad to see you.

RALEIGH: They'll think I gave up.

MAY: No. They'll be glad you didn't go fight. They'll be real glad to see you.

RALEIGH: Later. After I've been in New York City for a while.

MAY: Don't you miss Kentucky? I missed Corbin. When I was in California.

RALEIGH: Corbin's a nice town. The Nibroc festival.

MAY: I've never been.

RALEIGH: You've never been to the Nibroc festival?

MAY: No.

RALEIGH: And you grew up in Corbin.

MAY: Yes.

RALEIGH: Lived in Corbin all your life?

MAY: Yes.

RALEIGH: And you've never been to the Nibroc festival?

MAY: No. Have you?

RALEIGH: Sure.

MAY: I haven't.

RALEIGH: Why not?

MAY: I always went to the tent meeting. It's the same time of year. I went to the tent meetings at the campgrounds. To hear all the preachers.

RALEIGH: You "saved"?

MAY: Of course. You?

RALEIGH: Baptist. I've been baptized. Don't have to keep being saved.

MAY: It's not exactly like that.

RALEIGH: A person doesn't have to stand up every time they hear the call, every time they hear "Lamb of God."

MAY: I don't.

RALEIGH: I never understood why people get saved all over again every summer.

MAY: I guess they have to, after the Nibroc festival. They go to the Nibroc festival, then they have to be saved again.

RALEIGH: You're wrong about that.

MAY: It just seems to me.

RALEIGH: The festival's not like that. Some people, some boys get a little moonshine, maybe, but mostly it's just to get people together. And elect the queen. The queen of the festival. It's like a fair.

MAY: I know what it's like.

RALEIGH: No, you don't. You haven't been.

MAY: I'm from Corbin. I know what the Nibroc festival is. You're not from Corbin. You don't know.

RALEIGH: I've been, though. I've been to the festival. And I'm going to take you to the festival.

MAY: No, you're not.

RALEIGH: Yes, I am. Next year I am going to take you to the Nibroc festival.

MAY: I thought you were going to New York City.

(A pause.)

RALEIGH: I'm going to New York City and then I'm going to take you to the Nibroc festival.

MAY: If you go to New York City you won't be coming home to take me anywhere. People who go away, change. They're not like from home anymore.

RALEIGH: Like your fiancé.

MAY: Like him. Yes, like him.

RALEIGH: I was in California, too.

MAY: Well, I didn't know you before.

RALEIGH: You're starting to know me now.

MAY: We're just riding this train together. That's all.

(May starts reading her book. A pause.)

RALEIGH: There aren't any other seats that I can see, but if I catch sight of anyone getting off at the next station I'll try to move.

MAY: You don't have to.

RALEIGH: I don't like to sit where I'm not welcome. I'll move just as soon as I can and some woman with a wailing baby will take my place. Well, I'm going to go ride back with the coffins. With F. Scott and Nathanael West.

MAY: Don't be silly.

RALEIGH: Is that a smile? No, couldn't be. Yep, I'd better go ride back there with the writers. The dead writers.

MAY: Stop.

RALEIGH: Old F. Scott and young Nat.

MAY: That's morbid.

RALEIGH: Scotty and Natty.

MAY: *(Suppressing a giggle in spite of herself.)* Scotty and Natty?

RALEIGH: Well, now. You're going home. See, you should be happy. Another few hours and you can change trains for Kentucky.

MAY: You, too.

RALEIGH: Nope. I'm staying. On the train. Going to New York City. Funny, when I got on, boarded the train, back in Los Angeleese, I was going home. Not happy about it, but going home. I got on this train. Thought, I can go anywhere. Chicago, anywhere. No one's expecting me. No one knows I'm coming. Got a uniform still on, got a pass. Anywhere I want to go.

MAY: Well, I could go anywhere, too.

RALEIGH: You wanting to?

MAY: I don't know. Hadn't thought about it.

RALEIGH: Well, I have. I can go anywhere. Thought about Detroit, lots of work in the factories, my brother-in-law says, but I can go do that any time.

MAY: You don't want to go home?

RALEIGH: Nope. Home'll always be there. I got on this train, and the conductor told me that the coffins were being loaded in. That Nathaniel West and F. Scott Fitzgerald were riding the same train I was. So, don't you see, I can't let that go by. When would something like that ever happen again?

MAY: You didn't know them.

RALEIGH: I didn't know you, either, but now we're riding the same train. And no matter what happens, there will always have been a time that we rode the train together. Things are affected by other things. And I can't let it go by. That I'm on the train with the two greatest writers of this century. And I thought I've just got to stay on this train. Follow those men. This is my chance, my time, and if I don't take it now, don't move right now, not later, now, while I'm supposed to, it'll never happen again.

MAY: But you didn't know them.

RALEIGH: Sure I know them! I know everything they've written. Feels like I know them better than I know myself, even. And something real deep inside — I don't usually just spill everything out like this. *(A pause.)* I know your feller. Your fiancé.

(May stares at him.)

RALEIGH: Not well, but I know him. I've seen your picture. He didn't get leave. I had to stay. To get ready to be discharged. Buddies got leave. For Christmas. I had to stay for processing.

MAY: They got time off?

RALEIGH: They got leave.

MAY: And he didn't?

RALEIGH: Reckon not.

MAY: How come?

RALEIGH: Must not've earned it. Must not've worked hard enough.

MAY: So I had to miss Christmas with my family? So I had to come all the way out here because he's lazy?

RALEIGH: I really don't know. Maybe he wanted you to come because he thought you'd have a good time.

MAY: Well, he was wrong. I had a terrible time. He was different and he smoked and he didn't have any place for me to stay.

RALEIGH: Housing is getting tight, hard to —

MAY: Why'd he have me come out?

RALEIGH: Don't know. I don't know him very well.

MAY: And I slept on this porch, this woman's porch. Didn't really sleep, couldn't sleep, it was a porch. A porch in a strange place.

RALEIGH: Were you cold?

MAY: No, but it was just a porch.

RALEIGH: Don't you sleep on the porch back home? When it's hot?

MAY: Well, yes.

RALEIGH: A porch is a porch.

MAY: This was in a stranger's house. Not even the house. The porch. This woman I didn't know.

RALEIGH: Well, where did you want to sleep? A hotel?

MAY: Of course not! Not unless we, if we were —

RALEIGH: Were you planning to get married? Out there?

MAY: I don't know! It seemed — I just went because he — I don't know. And then it just wasn't the same. He's different.

RALEIGH: Everyone's different. Everyone's changing. The world's changed. You've changed.

MAY: You never knew me.

RALEIGH: No, but I'll just bet you've changed. Going all the way across the country on a train. Something's got to be different when you get back. *(A pause.)* You going to need my handkerchief again?

MAY: No, I'm not.

RALEIGH: It's here if you need it.

MAY: I don't.

RALEIGH: Well, just in case, it's here.

MAY: I wouldn't take your hanky if this train went through the Johnstown flood.

RALEIGH: Little missy, this trip of yours has sure made you feisty. Bet they won't even know you back in Corbin. You'll march into the Dixie Dog and they'll hand you the catsup without you even asking.

MAY: He's the one changed.

RALEIGH: Think so?

MAY: Know so.

RALEIGH: So.

(An uncomfortable pause.)

MAY: I'm going to read now. If you don't mind.

RALEIGH: Be my guest. Back to your *Magnificent Obsession*.

MAY: Don't tell me the ending.

RALEIGH: You'll have to find out for yourself.

(Raleigh starts to stand up.)

MAY: Going to the smoking car?

RALEIGH: That's right.

MAY: Don't come back smelling of smoke.

RALEIGH: I don't smoke.

MAY: In that case maybe I'll save your seat.

RALEIGH: Thanks. I'd like that.

(Raleigh turns to go up the aisle.)

MAY: Wait. What did he say about me?

RALEIGH: Your feller? He said you were a goody-two-shoes.

MAY: *(Pause.)* You think I'm a goody-two-shoes?

RALEIGH: I think you think you are.

MAY: That's the same thing.

RALEIGH: Nope. I think deep down inside you have an adventurous spirit. Not every girl from Corbin, Kentucky, would get on a train and ride all the way to California not knowing what she was going to find there. Not many girls would talk to a soldier she didn't even know and cry in his handkerchief.

MAY: I'm going to be a missionary.

RALEIGH: Excuse me?

MAY: I told him. I've always wanted to be a missionary. He knew that. I wanted us to be missionaries.

RALEIGH: I said you had an adventurous spirit.

MAY: That's not adventurous.

RALEIGH: You don't like sleeping on a porch. Think you're going to like living in a hut?

MAY: I won't sleep in a hut.

RALEIGH: You sure will. Missionaries live in huts.

MAY: I hadn't thought about it.

RALEIGH: I reckon you hadn't thought about it. Well, you better be thinking about it. Think you were going to live on a plantation with native servants?

MAY: Not exactly.

RALEIGH: Doesn't your church pack up barrels with used clothes for the missionaries?

MAY: Well, yes.

RALEIGH: You'd be getting a barrel full of old clothes to hang up in your hut. It's a hard life for a woman.

MAY: I live on a farm. I can hoe a row, shuck corn, milk a cow and wring a chicken's neck.

RALEIGH: And I had you pegged for a town girl.

MAY: Just outside of town. Off highway twenty-five.

RALEIGH: North or south?

MAY: North.

RALEIGH: T'wards London.

MAY: Yes. Off twenty-five.

RALEIGH: You know the Logans?

MAY: Live across the road. They're neighbors.

RALEIGH: Cousins. I'm cousins with them. I know your farm. Nice piece of land.

MAY: It's —

RALEIGH: Not bottom land, like Raccoon Creek, but not too hilly.

MAY: We've got lots of blackberries.

RALEIGH: I love blackberries.

MAY: Me, too.

RALEIGH: I'll come pick blackberries on your farm and we'll go to the Nibroc festival. Unless you're off in some jungle converting the natives.

MAY: That will be a while. I just finished school. In Wilmore.

RALEIGH: Asbury College. Church school. So you're serious about this missionary work.

MAY: Of course I am.

RALEIGH: I thought you were just making it up.

MAY: Oh, no. I've been serious about it for a long time. I'm serious. I think.

RALEIGH: You think? You'd better think. It must be a hard life. Lonely. No one you know around. Nobody to speak your language with. Except a husband. *(A pause.)* You have to be married to be a missionary, don't you?

MAY: I think so.

RALEIGH: So, it'll be a while before you go away.

MAY: I suspect so.

RALEIGH: Why don't you come with me to New York City?

MAY: Excuse me?

RALEIGH: Come to New York City.

MAY: I don't know anyone in New York City.

RALEIGH: You know me. There's women's boarding houses. I've read about them.

MAY: Maybe you read too much.

RALEIGH: Maybe.

MAY: I could never live in a city.

RALEIGH: Have you ever been to one?

MAY: Silly. I just came from Los Angelees.

RALEIGH: That's not a real city.

MAY: I've been to Louisville *(Pronounced "L'LL-v'lle".)*. I don't like Louisville.

RALEIGH: I wanted to go to Paris. With the war. And London. That's why I volunteered. London, England, not Kentucky. So if I can't go to Europe I'll go to New York City.

MAY: Well, I'm going home to Kentucky. And so should you.

RALEIGH: I'm going to New York City. Going to be a writer. When I'm a writer then I can go back home.

MAY: It won't be the same.

RALEIGH: It's not the same now. We're all changing. We're all riding this country's future like this train's a'rolling along the track, just hoping we get somewhere and don't run off the tracks somewhere along the way. Trusting that the engineer and the brakeman and the signalman are all on the job, trusting that they'll get us there in one piece.

MAY: That's very poetic.

RALEIGH: Told you I was a writer.

MAY: So you did.

RALEIGH: Now prove to me that you're a missionary. Pray something for us. Pray that we get to where we're supposed to go. Pray that we don't go to war.

MAY: I'm having a hard time praying these days.

RALEIGH: Okay. I'll leave you alone.

(A pause.)

MAY: I'm sorry I said those things.

RALEIGH: Which things are you sorry you said?

MAY: Well, about the porch. It wasn't so bad.

RALEIGH: Those things.

MAY: You keep teasing me.

RALEIGH: Just looking for the brighter side. *(A pause.)* Come to New York City.

MAY: With you? I don't do things like that.

RALEIGH: There's lady's boarding houses in New York City. Lots of jobs.

MAY: No. I'm not . . . brave.

RALEIGH: You're very brave.

MAY: I'm not at all brave. I'm a scaredy-cat. I'm a whipped pup, going home with my tail between my legs. I'm silly. I'm timid. I'm not at all brave.

RALEIGH: I think you're brave.

MAY: 'Cause I want to be a missionary?

RALEIGH: Wanting something's not brave. If you become a missionary, I reckon that would be brave, but giving it up is brave, too. Giving up one dream for another is brave. Oh, you gotta read Nathanael West. Everyday-ordinary things are brave sometimes. Talking to strangers like me is brave. Going to California took courage, and leaving it took even more.

MAY: I hadn't thought about it. I've mostly just been feeling bad.

RALEIGH: You should feel good about, well, about escaping that fate.

MAY: Is going to New York City brave?

RALEIGH: Of course it is!

MAY: Being a soldier is brave.

RALEIGH: Not being a soldier, flyer, is braver.

MAY: Why aren't you gonna be a flyer any more?

RALEIGH: Discharge. Medical discharge.

MAY: Why?

RALEIGH: I started getting the fits out there. *(May stares at him.)* Something sort of like the fits. Just a little bit. Once or twice only. But they're discharging me.

MAY: That's why you don't want to go home. *(A very long pause as May doesn't quite know what to say.)* You can always go to New York City later, if you really want to.

RALEIGH: But now's my opportunity.

MAY: Following dead men. Going to New York City because there's some dead men going there?

RALEIGH: They're famous writers.

MAY: They *were* famous writers, or so you say. I've never heard of one of them.

RALEIGH: He's famous.

MAY: But they're dead.

RALEIGH: They're famous writers.

MAY: But they're dead. It's over for them. Not you. Having a couple of little fits won't kill you. So why're you following dead men? Can't visit them in New York City. And are those coffins even going to New York City? Isn't your friend Mr. Fitzgerald going to Virginia or Delaware or someplace?

RALEIGH: Maryland.

MAY: See? What'd he write about, anyway?

RALEIGH: Rich people, flappers.

MAY: Rich people where?

RALEIGH: The Riviera and New York City and —

MAY: He wrote about New York City.

RALEIGH: Yep.

MAY: So what are you going to write about?

RALEIGH: Stories.

MAY: About what?

RALEIGH: People.

MAY: People where?

RALEIGH: In the mountains.

MAY: In Kentucky.

RALEIGH: Yep.

MAY: So why are you going to New York City if you're going to write about Kentucky?

(Raleigh is taken aback. A pause.)

RALEIGH: That's where writers go. New York City.

MAY: Are they happy there? You think Mr. Fitzgerald was happy in New York City?

RALEIGH: No.

MAY: Were you happy in Kentucky? You miss it?

RALEIGH: Yes, of course.

MAY: I don't have to say any more.

RALEIGH: No, I reckon you don't, little miss.

MAY: Excuse me, mister.

RALEIGH: My mistake. Taking this seat.

MAY: You can tease the dog but you don't like its bark.

(A long pause. Raleigh looks at May for a moment.)

RALEIGH: Yes, I do. Like its bark. *(A pause.)* My name's Raleigh. Nice to meet you.

MAY: *(Offering her hand.)* Oh. I'm May. Nice to meet you.

RALEIGH: Well, May, I've got a question for you.

MAY: What is it?

RALEIGH: Well, if I come back to Kentucky —

MAY: When?

RALEIGH: Now. If I change trains with you, when you do —

MAY: You thinking about it?

RALEIGH: I'm thinking about it.

MAY: *(Teasing.)* It'd be a brave thing to do. Going to Kentucky. Brave.

RALEIGH: That's enough.

MAY: Sorry.

RALEIGH: As I was saying, May —

MAY: Yes, Raleigh.

RALEIGH: You got a mouth on you, you know.

MAY: Never had before. Guess I got too much sun in California.

RALEIGH: Well, anyway, if I go to Kentucky.

MAY: Yes.

RALEIGH: Hush, now, I want to say this.

MAY: All right.

RALEIGH: No, hush. *(A pause.)* I know you're just getting over, that you don't know. I mean about the missionary work — that you'll be, well, I reckon, do you — if I come home, haven't decided yet, mind you, but if I do, or when — Could I take you to the Nibroc festival?

MAY: Ask me when you're home.

RALEIGH: No, *now*, say I'm going home. I mean, that's home, say I'm going there. Will you go to the Nibroc festival with me?

MAY: *(Pause.)* No.

(A long pause.)

RALEIGH: Why not?

MAY: It's heathen.

RALEIGH: What? What do you mean?

MAY: People probably drinking. And dances. And beauty contests.

RALEIGH: That's heathen?

MAY: Well, no, but its name.

RALEIGH: Nibroc?

MAY: After some heathen god or something.

RALEIGH: What do you mean? It's not named after —

MAY: Or something heathen.

RALEIGH: Nibroc is Corbin spellt backwards.

MAY: No.

RALEIGH: Spell it out.

MAY: I never knew that. I never thought about it before. I never went.

RALEIGH: It's just a big party, May.

MAY: Funny how you grow up with things —

RALEIGH: Yeah. Funny.

MAY: You come back to Kentucky and I'll go to the Nibroc festival with you.

RALEIGH: Really?

MAY: Yes, I'll go. But I won't go alone.

RALEIGH: I should think not. Well, then, maybe I'll just have to take you.

MAY: What about your friends in the coffins back there?

RALEIGH: They're "different from you and me."

(Blackout.)

MEN'S
Bob Jude Ferrante
Man & Woman

Scene: A men's room.

Colleen (twenty to thirty), a woman deserted by her boyfriend, and Mac (thirties), a man just trying to take care of business.

When Colleen encounters Mac while searching for her boyfriend in the men's room, she finds a sympathetic ear, and a little bit of hope for the future.

The door to a men's room. Colleen stands at the door. She hesitates. She moves to knock, then hesitates again. Finally she gets up the gumption and hits the door, then ducks out of the way. Brief pause. She comes back to the door and hits it three times, hard. Silence. Now she starts pounding on the door.

COLLEEN: Gerry! Gerry get your ass out here! Gerry!
(The door opens and Mac stands in the doorway.)
MAC: Hey! Lady! Hey!
COLLEEN: What?!
MAC: Can't a guy take a whizz in peace?
COLLEEN: I'm sorry.
MAC: You should be.
COLLEEN: Well I am.
MAC: Fine.
(Looks at her for a moment, then turns to leave.)
COLLEEN: There wasn't . . .
(Mac turns to her.)
MAC: What?
COLLEEN: Um . . . another man in there with you . . . was there?
MAC: Lady, I didn't notice. I mean, I usually try not to. You know what I mean?
COLLEEN: Oh, yeah. I know *exactly* what you mean.

MAC: Well, I'm glad we understand each other. *(Pause.)* I guess I could check.

COLLEEN: Really?

MAC: Yeah, I will if you want me to.

COLLEEN: You don't have to.

MAC: I'm volunteerin' right here where I stand.

COLLEEN: That's so nice of you! And after I interfered with your . . . and all.

MAC: What's he look like? This guy Gerry?

COLLEEN: Oh yeah. I was saying his name.

MAC: You was *screamin'* his name. So?

COLLEEN: About . . . your height. Black hair. Blue eyes.

MAC: Celtic.

COLLEEN: Celtic?

MAC: Black hair, blue eyes. That's what I am.

COLLEEN: And kind of muscular. Also like you.

MAC: Ha. So maybe . . . you're looking for me?

COLLEEN: No. *(Slight pause.)* I mean, I'm sorry, please don't take this the wrong way.

MAC: It's OK. I'm a big boy, I can take it. I'll be right back.

(Mac turns to go into the men's room.)

COLLEEN: We were having a fight.

(Mac turns back again.)

MAC: Sorry to hear that. What was yas fightin' about?

COLLEEN: I don't know. Whatever shit you fight about . . . sorry.

MAC: Yas can say 'shit.' I don't give a fuck . . . so?

(They both laugh.)

COLLEEN: It's kind of personal.

MAC: OK. I'll be right back. *(Mac turns to go in.)* Yo, Gerry, I'm comin' in!

(Mac goes in. Pause.)

COLLEEN: Well? *(Silence.)* Do you see him?

MAC: *(From off.)* Yo, Gerry! *(Silence. Finally Mac pokes his head out.)* Ain't nobody in there, lady.

COLLEEN: Colleen.

(Mac steps out of the door.)

MAC: Dat's a beautiful name.

COLLEEN: Thanks.

MAC: It's Celtic, too. Like mine.

COLLEEN: I could really give a shit about name etymology.

(Colleen cries softly. Mac stands over her awkwardly.)

MAC: What do you think happened to him?

COLLEEN: We were just looking at the menus, and he was telling me about Madrid. He said he had a lot of work, and his company couldn't pay to take me along. I told him, It's OK, I could pay. Then he said he had to go to the . . . oh God!

(Mac takes out a hankie.)

MAC: Shit. That's tough, Colleen.

COLLEEN: Tough! You don't know anything about tough! This keeps happening to me! I used to date this guy Philip. He said he loved me and he was going to leave his wife. So he left me standing in an airport holding tickets to Antigua. I call his house, and he and his wife are away on a camping trip.

MAC: Oh, man.

COLLEEN: But that's only one example. I've been left standing at an ATM after handing a boyfriend a thousand dollars to pay off his phone bill. In East Harlem at midnight waiting for a Jazz concert. Outside a steak restaurant in the biggest hurricane to hit the East Coast in 20 years. You name it, some guy's stood me up in front of it, beside it, in it, or on it! And now, outside a fucking men's room!

MAC: It's clean.

(Colleen blows her nose loudly.)

Yas can keep it.

COLLEEN: Thanks.

(Pause.)

COLLEEN: Maybe you can tell me what you'd do. Suppose you were going away on business for a month. Would you take your wife?

MAC: No.

COLLEEN: Figures!

MAC: 'Cause she's dead.

COLLEEN: Oh, Jesus! I'm sorry!

MAC: A year ago.

(Slight pause. Colleen sits on the floor.)

So yas was askin', if I was married, or while I was married, or whatever, what would I do.

COLLEEN: I don't know any more.

MAC: No, Colleen. It's easy. A no-braina. If I was gonna be away for a month, and someplace interestin' . . .

COLLEEN: Madrid.

MAC: Like Madrid. If I loved that woman, and believe me I was totally and utterly in love with my wife, then you bet your ass, I would take her.

(Pause.)

COLLEEN: I'm sorry about the crack I made. About your name.

MAC: It's OK. You're hurtin'. I unnerstan'.

COLLEEN: What is it? Your name?

MAC: Mac.

COLLEEN: Really?

MAC: Yeah. It's like, people know my name automatically. "What's your problem, Mac?" "Hey, Mac, you got a light?"

COLLEEN: *(Laughs.)* Pretty handy.

MAC: Fuck yeah. And speakin' of handy, it's also a computer. And a raincoat. All in all, I'm a pretty useful guy.

(Pause.)

COLLEEN: I'm sorry I banged on the door and disturbed you.

MAC: Some guys can't . . . you know.

COLLEEN: What?

MAC: Take a whiz. If there's too much noise. Laugh if you want. It's called "nervous bladder."

COLLEEN: Oh, no. I'm not laughing.

MAC: So . . . uh . . . how long was you two goin' out?

COLLEEN: Three months.

MAC: And he . . . uh . . . ever take off on you before? *(Slight pause.)* I'm sorry. That ain't really the question to —

COLLEEN: — No, it's OK. Yeah, actually, he does, whenever we don't agree, he just . . . *(Pause.)* That's kind of why I got up so fast . . . and sort of hung out here, by the . . . because he . . . *(Colleen starts crying again.)* And I was just telling him . . .

MAC: What?

COLLEEN: I'm . . .

MAC: You're kidding. Pregnant?

(Colleen nods.)

Jesus! I mean, forgive me for sayin' this.

COLLEEN: Go ahead.

MAC: I mean, he souns like a real friggin' son of a bitch, if you ask me. Not like the kind of guy a beautiful woman like you should be seein'. If I'm goin' too far here, you can disagree.

COLLEEN: No. I agree so far.

(Long pause.)

MAC: My wife was . . . she was pregnant. When she died. Complications in childbirth.

(Colleen stands and starts to put her arms around him.)

COLLEEN: Oh, Jesus, Mac. I'm sorry.

MAC: That's just it. I got over all of it. I don't think about the slippers I used to trip over every morning, or the sink fulla dishes, or movie popcorn.

COLLEEN: What's wrong with movie popcorn?

MAC: Emily, she used to say only movie theatre popcorn tasted good. She used to send me out into the night. I used to beg the guy to let me into the lobby so's I could pay five bucks for a tub of popcorn.

COLLEEN: You must have really loved her.

MAC: Yeah. Popcorn. That grease they put on it . . . butta flavor.

(Laughs to himself.)

Uh. So you guys order?

COLLEEN: No, we didn't get a . . .

MAC: Well then. Might a gentleman ask a lady out for a bite to eat?

COLLEEN: Uh.

(Brushes herself off.)

I . . . uh . . . sure.

MAC: Done.

(Pause.)

There's one small wrinkle.

COLLEEN: What?

MAC: I gotta step back in here a minute, I never got a chance to. Can you wait for me?

COLLEEN: Mac. I've already been stood up once tonight by a guy going to the bathroom. Please don't put me in that same situation again.

MAC: I'm not sure what choice I got.

COLLEEN: To prove you had good intentions, you could invite me in.

MAC: Ha! In the men's john?

(Pause.)

Is that . . . is that OK to do? It's the man's domain in here.

COLLEEN: According to Hoyle, if a gentleman invites a lady in, she can enter the man's . . . domain.

MAC: Listen, are you really sure of that? Because it seems kind of . . .

COLLEEN: Gerry was a lawyer.

(Brief pause.)

MAC: Looks like I got no choice, huh?

COLLEEN: Not if you want to go with me.

(Brief pause.)

MAC: Very well. Please step into my . . . domain, good lady.

COLLEEN: Don't mind if I do, kind sir.

(They go into the men's room together. Blackout.)

THE NEGRO OF PETER THE GREAT

Carlyle Brown

Man & Woman

Scene: The Court of Peter the Great of Russia.

Ibrahim (thirties), godson to Peter the Great, black, and Leonora (twenty to thirty), the countess he loves.

Ibrahim has been called back to Russia from Paris by the Csar. Here, he says farewell to Leonora, a married woman with whom he has sired a child.

LEONORA: What does it mean, Ibrahim?

IBRAHIM: The Czar wants me to return to Russia.

LEONORA: But the Czar has sent you these letters before and you didn't leave then. He says in this letter that it's up to you. He says he would never desert you. And he will continue sending you your allowance.

IBRAHIM: Allowance? What allowance? You call that pittance an allowance? That's just his Czarist Russian way of giving me an order. I have to go.

LEONORA: But why do you have to go? Look Ibrahim, I know how it must be difficult for you here. But as alien as you are in France, your long stay here was made you equally a stranger to the cold and common customs of half savage Russia. I know that the Duke of 'Orleans will give you permission to remain in France, for which you've already shed your blood. Stay Ibrahim. Stay here with me.

IBRAHIM: I haven't any money, Leonora.

LEONORA: We'll petition for a position. We'll sponsor you at court.

IBRAHIM: A title without land? That would be worthless.

LEONORA: Marriage to nobility can put that soil under your feet. There are many young girls in Paris who pray every day, that when they are given in marriage, they'll be given to a man like you.

IBRAHIM: Leonora, what shall I do? Marry some young girl and keep you as a lover? You would only hate it as I do. The secrets, lies, clandestine encounters. The thought of someone else lying in your bed. Touching you, kissing you, and the complete absence of any future between us. How could you bear it?

LEONORA: What I couldn't bear is not to have any encounters with you at all. I pray I never have to choose. Yes, it's been difficult for us, I know. But we've been spared the scandal, the gossip is dying down. We're safe.

IBRAHIM: Safe? How can we be safe? Here, I have a gift for you. A handkerchief I picked up in the woods. I met a young French cavalry officer in the field this morning.

LEONORA: A duel? You're not hurt?

IBRAHIM: And it wasn't just my honor he insulted.

LEONORA: Tell me you're not hurt.

IBRAHIM: It was you. He insulted you. It was for your sake that I took up his glove.

LEONORA: Ibrahim, how could you? I begged you never to defend me. A scandal will dishonor me more than any insult. Or what if something should happen to you? I don't want you risking your life for my sake. And now people could start to talk all over again.

IBRAHIM: A soldier's world is not polite society. A musket ball was the only way to assure his discretion.

LEONORA: Is he dead?

IBRAHIM: What does it matter? It only proves that I have to go.

LEONORA: But, why do you have to go?

IBRAHIM: Sooner or later your husband is bound to discover us. What if he should call me out?

LEONORA: He wouldn't dare. He knows your skill. It would be certain death.

IBRAHIM: Fate always has a certain hand to play in these things. But whatever it is, whatever his fears, whatever his feelings, he's a gentleman. He has no choice. He must protect his honor.

LEONORA: Then you must refuse him.

IBRAHIM: My honor is as precious to me as his. My honor is all I have. What else is there to stand between me and complete oblivion, but my honor? I have neither a title or lands. I receive an allowance like some fop. I'm the Czar's Negro. I barely can claim my own name. My uniform is thread bare. I'm wretched. And this society, this frivolous society persecutes, pitilessly persecutes everything it claims it will allow in theory. It's just a matter of time before that cold, pompous derision, the insinuations, the deceit, will catch up to us. And what will become of us then?

Then you will become ashamed of me. Of us. Then your fascination with me will be finished.

LEONORA: Fascination? It isn't fascination. I love you, Ibrahim. You, for yourself.

IBRAHIM: It's bound to happen, Leonora. Society demands it. Whatever it is that is alien to them is considered to be repugnant and loathsome. I couldn't bear it Leonora, for you to find me repugnant, loathsome. So, I'm leaving.

LEONORA: Repugnant? Loathsome? You can't believe that? You can't really believe that I could ever feel that way? About you? I thought you knew me. And what will I do when you're gone? What will I think about or look forward to. What will I dream on or remember, if not for you? I know that there's nothing else for us, but to be lovers. But still, that's not just some trifle to me. We just must be more careful this time. We just must be more discreet, that's all.

IBRAHIM: Leonora, have you forgotten everything? All we've endured? The insults to your pride? The terrible birth of our son? That we were forced to exchange him?

LEONORA: Please Ibrahim, I don't want to talk about that. I don't want to think about our son. I can't.

IBRAHIM: I saw him today.

LEONORA: Our son? You saw the baby? You saw him?

IBRAHIM: Yes.

[COUNT L: *(From within.)* Leonora!]

LEONORA: Coming! . . . How is he?

IBRAHIM: He is as well as to be expected. He lives in a hovel in the worst part of Paris. I found him suckling on his new mother's breast. He's not as dark as he was when he was born. He's a little fawn colored now. His hair is curly and he has your eyes.

LEONORA: I was in despair. In utter misery. It all seemed so hopeless. We were going to be ruined. There was nothing else we could do. Yes, I complained bitterly. I wasn't strong, and when I couldn't see you, I brooded and was so absent minded and distracted. Then when you came I reproached you. Oh Ibrahim, darling, I'm so sorry.

IBRAHIM: How can you pretend that baby in there, that changeling, is your son? You and the Count. While to stop a scandal, our boy lives some miserable life somewhere, with some peasant woman, who we don't even know who she is.

LEONORA: I can barely look at that child in there now as it is. And the Count is convinced it's the spitting image of him. I know you think it was frivolous and capricious of me, Ibrahim. But a woman must secure her future in any way she can. But that has nothing to do with love.

IBRAHIM: There it is. Don't you see? You cannot leave your husband. You're safe. You have nothing to gain by being with me, and I have everything to lose.

[COUNT L: *(From within.)* Leonora!]

LEONORA: Yes, I'm coming!

IBRAHIM: Why should you? A woman like you, embrace your fate with a man people scarcely deign to recognize as human?

LEONORA: Ibrahim please, kiss me quickly.

NO. 11 (BLUE AND WHITE)

Alexandra Cunningham

Man & Woman

Scene: Suburban Connecticut.

Lindsay (sixteen), a high school student making bad choices, and Dad (forties), her disassociated father.

Following a late night out, Dad reveals his complete lack of understanding of Lindsay's life in the following conversation.

DAD: *(Jovial.)* Three minutes to one — this is a first. Congratulations.

LINDSAY: Thanks.

DAD: No, thank *you.* So how was it.

LINDSAY: What.

DAD: Your date. What'd you do?

LINDSAY: Oh, you know, nothing.

DAD: Nothing? You did *nothing.*

LINDSAY: Well, you know, we drove around, we went to . . . places, it was — whatever.

DAD: What's so great about that? You swan around in some kid's car, he doesn't even take you out to eat or anything —

LINDSAY: We *ate.*

DAD: Yeah? What. What'd you eat.

LINDSAY: . . . We went to Post Corner —

DAD: Oh, *yeah,* a couple greasy slices of shitty pizza — shitty *Greek* pizza, not even real Italian, why people go to Greek pizza joints is beyond me. You know, when I grew up in Syracuse we had the best Italian food. I'm telling you, the best, you couldn't *get* bad Italian food in upstate New York. We were spoiled. So you ate Greek pizza and drove around. That's it?

LINDSAY: . . . What?

DAD: When I was your age I was busy, All County Baseball, Regents Exams to study for, the *draft,* but when I made time to take a girl out, I did it right. Came to the door to pick her up, walked her *back* to the door to say good night. Made it an occasion. Otherwise, what's the point. I didn't hear a car in the driveway just now.

LINDSAY: He dropped me off at the circle, I walked from the circle.

DAD: He dropped you *off?*

LINDSAY: I walked. It was fine. It was fine.

DAD: He have somewhere else to go? He doesn't have the *time* to drive you all the way to your door, he drops you off halfway? Save a little time by making his date walk two blocks in the dark? You like guys who act like that? Seriously, I'm asking, 'cause I don't know.

LINDSAY: I wanted to walk. I wouldn't like it but I wanted to walk.

DAD: That's not how a gentleman behaves. I know there aren't any, anymore, there aren't any more gentlemen, but if there were, they wouldn't be caught dead letting their girlfriend walk a quarter of a mile in the dark. I swear, I could kill these little pissy-ass snotnoses. Pulling up here in their Mommy's Wagoneer and honking, they expect you to come running. Next time that little shit comes to pick you up, I'm gonna spread nails in the driveway .

LINDSAY: Dad?

DAD: Nails and tacks. That'll be a big surprise for that little jerk.

LINDSAY: *(Tiny.)* . . . Dad?

DAD: *(Spideysense finally kicking in partially.)* What? . . . What's the matter?

LINDSAY: . . . um, do we have any juice?

DAD: What is going on?

LINDSAY: Nothing. I'm going to bed.

DAD: . . . Good. Get some sleep . . . You're a beautiful girl, Lindsay. You know that? Back when I was in school they would have been lining up around the block. They'd take you anywhere you wanted to go. *And,* walk you to the door when it was over. You know that? Don't accept anything less.

LINDSAY: I know, you've said.

DAD: Having to sit here and listen to you tell me what passes for a date these days. How this guy treated you tonight. What passes for politeness, what you girls let them get away with. 'Cause you know, if you all put your foot down, this crap would stop. If you told them how you wanted to be treated, they'd have to go along with it. They would. Because they wouldn't have a choice.

LINDSAY: Yeah. Good night.

DAD: Good night. Don't put up with it, sweetheart. You know what I'm saying?

LINDSAY: Yeah. Good night.

NUMBER 76
David-Matthew Barnes
Man & Woman

Scene: A bus stop.

Mario (fifteen), Latin, struggling to help his suicidal and possibly pregnant girlfriend, Ana (fifteen).

As they wait for a bus, Mario and Ana confront the choices they've made and the grim options available to them.

ANA: I'm cold.

MARIO: It's okay, babe. I'm here.

ANA: Maybe the bus broke down.

MARIO: It'll be here soon.

ANA: It's okay. I don't mind waiting.

MARIO: As long as we're together, right?

ANA: I don't want to go home.

MARIO: Where else are we gonna go?

ANA: I have seven dollars. My Tia Olivia gave it to me when I watched her bratty kids. I saved it.

MARIO: Seven dollars ain't much, babe.

ANA: Not enough to live on, I guess.

MARIO: Not even close.

ANA: Do you know Natasha Muñoz? She's in my science class.

MARIO: Does she go out with Ernesto?

ANA: No — she goes out with this black guy.

MARIO: I don't know her.

ANA: She wants to kick my ass.

MARIO: How come?

ANA: Because she likes you.

MARIO: I don't even know her, babe.

ANA: Well, she knows you. She said she'd fight me next week.

MARIO: I don't want you fightin' no more.

ANA: Because of the baby?

MARIO: We don't know for sure yet.

ANA: I know. I can feel it inside of me.

MARIO: Let's wait 'til we go to the doctor tomorrow.

ANA: Okay — but if I'm not pregnant — then I'm kickin' her ass. She's been messin' with me for three weeks now.

MARIO: She's just trippin'.

ANA: Are you sure you don't know her?

MARIO: I never heard of her.

ANA: She said that she kissed you two weeks ago at Junior's party. Remember — I couldn't go because I felt sick — so you went without me. Did you meet her there, Mario?

MARIO: No, babe. I've never met her.

ANA: She's kind of pretty, but she got a big nose.

MARIO: Nobody is as pretty as you are.

ANA: You're just sayin' that.

MARIO: I mean it —

ANA: You're just sayin' that because I might be pregnant with your baby.

MARIO: We'll find out tomorrow.

ANA: And then what?

MARIO: And then we will figure out what to do.

ANA: You know what, I'll probably have the baby a month before my birthday. Wouldn't that be cool?

MARIO: Sure, babe.

ANA: I'm still cold.

MARIO: Move closer to me.

ANA: *(Laughs a little.)* I can't get any closer.

MARIO: If we were naked —

ANA: I would freeze to death.

MARIO: I would keep you warm.

ANA: You always do.

MARIO: Ana, my angel.

ANA: Mario, my man.

MARIO: You wanna get married — if you're pregnant, I mean?

ANA: Of course.

MARIO: Cool.

ANA: And if I'm not pregnant?

MARIO: Well, then we'll wait — until we finish school and stuff.

ANA: I hope I'm pregnant.

MARIO: Me, too.

ANA: If it's a girl, Mario, I want to name her after your mother.

MARIO: Let's not talk about that.

ANA: But your Mom — she was the only person who was ever nice to me — besides you, I mean. Remember when she made me that dress? It was so pretty, Mario. She was always doing stuff like that for me.

MARIO: My mother was a good person.

ANA: Wow — I can't believe that we're saying was. It's only been a month.

MARIO: *(He suddenly gets up.)* That bus is fuckin' late.

ANA: Like I said — maybe it broke down.

MARIO: No, it'll be here.

ANA: Things break down all the time, Mario.

MARIO: I need to get home, Ana.

ANA: I can go with you. I can cook dinner for you and your brothers. And if your Dad is there —

MARIO: He won't be there.

ANA: Maybe he'll come home this time.

MARIO: He's never there.

ANA: I didn't see him, Mario. At the funeral. He should have been there to say good-bye.

MARIO: I don't wanna talk about it.

ANA: Come sit down with me.

MARIO: I'm looking for the bus.

ANA: I don't wanna go home.

MARIO: I know that.

ANA: If I had the money —

MARIO: Well, we don't.

ANA: We could go away somewhere.

MARIO: Where we gonna go, Ana?

ANA: We could go to California.

MARIO: What are we gonna do there?

ANA: I could open a flower shop. People like flowers. I could sell roses and daisies and white carnations.

MARIO: We have to finish school. And I can't leave my brothers. They need me right now.

ANA: I know. I guess I'm just trippin'. I just don't wanna go home.

MARIO: Is your step-dad still messin' with you?

ANA: Yeah — and my Mom knows about it. She just ignores it. Like everything else.

MARIO: I hate that fucking bastard.

ANA: Not as much as I do.

MARIO: *(Cautiously.)* Is that why you did it, Ana?

ANA: What are you talking about?

MARIO: When you tried to kill yourself.

ANA: Your mother always wanted to go to California. She told me before she — died. And she liked flowers too, Mario. That day she made me that dress and she gave it to me — she told me that your father never brought her flowers.

MARIO: I asked you a question.

ANA: Answer mine first.

MARIO: You didn't ask me anything.

ANA: How come you didn't go to the funeral?

MARIO: Why did you try to kill yourself?

ANA: I was there. I was holding hands with your brothers and I wore the dress. I kept looking down at it — at the buttons. And I was trippin' because your Mom made that thing for me with her own hands. It was like she loved me or somethin'. But your Dad wasn't there. And I wondered that if I died — would you be there? Would you wear that sweater that I made for you last Christmas?

MARIO: I didn't go to the funeral because my mother wanted to die.

ANA: I couldn't take the bullshit anymore. It's as simple that. My step-dad and my idiot mother. I just wanted to go away, Mario.

MARIO: And leave me?

ANA: I didn't do it because of you.

MARIO: Don't I love you enough, Ana?

ANA: You'll love me more if I'm pregnant.

MARIO: I've been taking care of you for two years.

ANA: You'll get tired of me soon.

MARIO: How can you say that?

ANA: Or maybe you already have.

MARIO: Ana, I love you.

ANA: *(Outburst.)* I was at the fucking party, Mario! I saw you with her!

MARIO: What?

ANA: I got to Junior's party late. But you were already there. You were in a bedroom with Natasha Muñoz — fucking her brains out! I saw you through the window, Mario. I saw you with her!

MARIO: Ana, I'm sorry.

ANA: You said you didn't know her!

MARIO: I don't. She was just there — and we —

ANA: How could you do this to me?!

MARIO: It was right after you tried to kill yourself.

ANA: I tried to kill myself because I was sick and tired of my step-dad coming in to my room in the middle of the night. I did it because my mother is a lying bitch who hates my guts. I took those pills because I knew that no matter how much I loved you — it wouldn't matter. Because you would get bored of me and fuck some whore like that bitch at Junior's party. But I fucked up — because I didn't take enough and you crawled in my bedroom window and found me.

MARIO: I called the ambulance.

ANA: Did you call the ambulance when your mother did it? When you found her in the kitchen?

MARIO: She wanted to die.

ANA: So did I! But you wouldn't let me.

MARIO: Because I love you. I love you because you're my girlfriend and we come from the same neighborhood. And you might be pregnant with my kid.

ANA: I got my period last night, Mario.

MARIO: You mean —

ANA: I'm not pregnant. So — if you wanna leave me and go off with Natasha — go ahead. Junior's been coming by my house sometimes and he likes me. He said if you did me wrong, he'd fuck you up for my honor. Then he'd be with me.

MARIO: Did you mess around with him?

ANA: He wanted me to. He was standing in my bedroom and he unbuckled his belt and unzipped his pants. It was just like —

MARIO: Me?

ANA: My step-dad. You ever notice how Junior and my step-dad — they've got the same smile. All evil and shit. I told Junior to get out because you were comin' over to pick me up and that you and I had to go fix dinner for your brothers because your drunk father got locked up again and I needed to be a good girlfriend to you because of your Mom. Junior said you were a punk ass bitch and you didn't know how to treat a girl and that it only took you five minutes to fuck Natasha.

MARIO: I didn't want to do it.

ANA: But she's all sprung on you now and thinks you're the fucking king of the *barrio* and shit like that. You can have that nasty bitch. She wouldn't have gone to your mother's funeral.

MARIO: I didn't go because I was happy for my mom. She finally got away from my dad.

ANA: But you didn't even cry.

MARIO: Why should I? It doesn't do any good to cry.

ANA: I always cry.

MARIO: That's because you feel too much.

ANA: *(Her mood suddenly shifts. She is much softer now, almost as if she were wounded.)* I'm cold.

MARIO: *(He goes to her, sits next to her and holds her.)* It's okay, babe. I'm here. Bus will be here soon.

ANA: I don't wanna go home, Mario.

MARIO: I know. Me either.

(As Ana is lost in her own thoughts, staring in a deep gaze, Mario reaches for her. She takes him into her arms and she holds him tightly. He begins to whimper as he finally cries.)

ANA: *(Comforting him.)* I don't wanna go home.

(Lights fade.)

PHONE PLAY
Edith Tarbescu
Man & Woman

Scene: Here and now.

Tom (twenties) and Pegi (twenties), a playful young couple.

Here, Pegi puts Tom's love to a very unique test on their six-week anniversary.

TOM: *(Entering living room, then drops his briefcase.)* Can you talk to me *now?*

PEGI: *(Quickly picking up her cellular phone.)* Okay, now I can. How was your trip?

TOM: Good — When did this start? This business of being able to talk to me only over the phone?

PEGI: I don't know. I think it started at work.

TOM: Well, it's crazy . . .

PEGI: Are you calling me crazy?

TOM: No, I'm not calling *you* crazy. But this . . . habit of yours. Are we only going to have phone sex, too?

PEGI: You are so inconsiderate. I'm practically having a nervous breakdown, and all you can think about is sex.

TOM: I'm only anticipating.

PEGI: Well, don't.

TOM: What happens if you put the phone down?

PEGI: I tried it when you walked through the door. I started having an anxiety attack.

TOM: Maybe that's because I came home early. I might have startled you.

PEGI: No, that wasn't why.

TOM: Is it just me? Or was it everybody you spoke to at work today ?

PEGI: It just seems to be you.

TOM: GREAT.

PEGI: Maybe it'll pass —

TOM: You mean like a — kidney stone?

PEGI: That was a disgusting image. I'm glad I found out what an optimist you are.

TOM: We've been living together for six weeks —

PEGI: And I just found out now. You've been clever at hiding your true self. I'm having a glass of wine. You want one?

TOM: Does that mean that while you're pouring, you can't talk to me?

PEGI: Under the circumstances, no. I can't pour wine and hold the phone at the same time.

TOM: Tuck it under your chin.

PEGI: The wine?

TOM: No, the phone.

PEGI: I can't. I might drop it.

TOM: You won't die.

PEGI: Thanks a lot —

TOM: You're making too much out of this. What if I just walked across the room and grabbed the phone away?

PEGI: You brute. You're just like my father. He used to do things like that.

TOM: Like what?

PEGI: Like grab things out of my hand. *(Facing him, pointedly.)* This phone is my security blanket.

TOM: I can't believe you just said that.

PEGI: My mother told me that until I was about three, I used to have this torn, raggedy blanket, but I loved it. And one day, my father just grabbed it away from me. I had nightmares about that for years.

TOM: So, twenty-three years later, you're still having a reaction?

PEGI: He also called me a cry-baby. He's a former Marine. I told you that. He always talked to me "man to man." I kept telling him I wasn't a boy. He said that didn't matter.

TOM: What about your mother? What did she do?

PEGI: She's a former Marine, too.

TOM: Can I have a drink? I don't want to just grab it out of your hand.

PEGI: Just a minute. I have a glass in one hand and my security blanket in the other. I have to put my wine down first —

TOM: Put the phone down —

PEGI: How could you be so insensitive? I just told you about one of the most traumatic experiences in my life and you ignore me. Are you an ex-Marine, too?

TOM: No. You *knew* me in college? Was I a Marine?

PEGI: No, but you joined ROTC.

TOM: That was to pay for college.

PEGI: So, you're almost an ex-Marine.

TOM: Almost doesn't count. *(Pause.)* Can I hold you? Would that help?

PEGI: If you don't make me put the phone down.

TOM: I won't make you put it down. I promise.

PEGI: Good. Because if you did that, I'd have to leave you.

TOM: Leave me? Why?

PEGI: Because you can't accept my eccentricities.

TOM: This isn't eccentric. It's nutty.

PEGI: Look, it happened while we were talking to each other at work. All of a sudden, I realized I wouldn't be able to talk to you without my cell phone.

TOM: That was at work. You *couldn't* talk to me any other way. We're home now — in our apartment — the one we picked out together.

PEGI: That's not exactly true. I wanted to live on the West Side.

TOM: But you agreed to the East Side.

PEGI: That's because I wanted to please you. I can't go on trying to please you forever.

TOM: So, you're rebelling by putting a phone between us.

PEGI: The phone is *not* between us.

TOM: Then, what is between us?

PEGI: Your lack of understanding.

TOM: Why don't you call your shrink?

PEGI: She's on vacation. You know that.

TOM: How 'bout calling Dr. Ruth?

PEGI: What does she know about phone fetishes? She's a sex doctor.

TOM: Well, if this continues, we're going to need her, so you might as well call her now.

PEGI: You are such a pessimist.

TOM: It's our six-week anniversary. I was planning to have some wine, call out for Chinese food. And make love to you.

PEGI: I won't be able to eat and talk at the same time. I'd have to put the phone down.

TOM: We'll take turns eating. I'll feed you.

PEGI: You'll feed yourself first; I know you. And my food'll get cold.

TOM: I'll feed you before I eat. How's that?

PEGI: *(Getting excited.)* Will you wear a Marine uniform?

TOM: NO. I will not. I don't even have one.

PEGI: I'll go out and rent one. There's a costume shop two blocks away.

TOM: Why should I wear a Marine uniform?

PEGI: Then I can reenact the trauma. And I'll get over my need for a security blanket.

TOM: Why don't I just grab it away ? That will reenact it better than anything.

PEGI: I knew you were insensitive from the first time I met you. You dropped a book. I bent to pick it up for you, and you looked at my boobs, instead of saying thank you.

TOM: You were wearing a see-through blouse.

PEGI: I was in college then.

TOM: So was I. Can I say a belated "thank you" for picking up my book?

PEGI: No, it's too late.

TOM: How can I make it up to you?

PEGI: You can't.

TOM: What happened at work today? Did something happen?

PEGI: No. I wrote some advertising copy. I handed it to my boss. She didn't particularly like it. And all of a sudden, I saw my father's face. That's when my phone rang —

TOM: The phone on your desk?

PEGI: No, the phone in my pocket. I *always* carry my cell phone with me. As soon as I picked it up, I imagined her grabbing it away from me. That's when it started. That's it . . . instead of a Marine uniform, dress as my boss —

TOM: IN DRAG? NO WAY.

PEGI: It's the only way I'll get over this fetish.

TOM: How do you know? Has it ever happened before?

PEGI: No. But I feel it. I sense it. I'm a very intuitive person.

TOM: What about me? What if cross-dressing becomes *my* fetish?

PEGI: It won't. I won't let it. Here. Let's try it at least.

(She puts down the phone, hands him a long, fringed scarf from a coatrack and a big, floppy hat.)

(Tom puts them on and starts prancing around.)

PEGI: You do love me. YOU DO.

TOM: You invented this whole thing as a test?

PEGI: Well . . . sort of.

TOM: I *love* this scarf. *(Dramatically, tosses it over his shoulder.)* We should play this game more often.

(Blackout.)

THE PRETTIEST GIRL
Ashley Leahy
Man & Woman

Scene: A party.

Angie and Frank (twenties), party guests.

Here, strangers meet over a plate of deviled eggs and their conversation reveals a strange memory.

ANGIE: You are beautiful. Everyone in the room is looking at you. Not because they see you as strange, but because you are the prettiest girl in the room.

FRANK: Excuse me, but could you put down the deviled eggs? The other guests might want to partake.

ANGIE: This man wants your advice on the universe. Look at how his left eyebrow is raised in disbelief. He cannot fathom how anyone could be so stunning. *(To Frank.)* Yes I will help you.

FRANK: Help me by giving me that tray.

ANGIE: You're smiling at me.

FRANK: No, I'm looking past you.

ANGIE: It's all right, no need to be afraid. *(She takes hold of his arm.)* You can touch my face. *(She places his hand on her cheek.)* Was it good for you?

FRANK: How long have you been a patient here?

ANGIE: *(Picking up a deviled egg and stuffing it into her mouth.)* I can't taste a thing.

FRANK: How many of those have you eaten?

ANGIE: Take two capsules daily on a full stomach.

FRANK: All right, eat the whole damn plate. See if I care. *(He turns to go.)*

ANGIE:He's leaving you. Not a good sign. *(To Frank.)* Wait.

FRANK: Why.

ANGIE: I just remembered where I know you from.

FRANK: Okay . . .

ANGIE: Halloween.

FRANK: I wasn't here on Halloween. *(He starts to leave.)*

ANGIE: Nor was I.

FRANK: Then what . . .

ANGIE: The movie. I was watching the movie *Halloween,* and I saw you. You walked into the theatre with a blonde lady. She looked like my sister. I remembered you because she looked like my sister.

FRANK: *(Trying to remember.)* I don't think . . .

ANGIE: Don't tell him what you did next. He'll forget you're beautiful. *(To Frank.)* It was you. You drove a green convertible.

FRANK: *(Remembers.)* I remember that day now. A girl was screaming and crying. It was my first date with Paula.

ANGIE: First dates are always magical.

FRANK: She was sitting a few rows behind us. I remember thinking it odd that she would scream and shout before the movie even began.

(Angie grows agitated, stuffs two more deviled eggs into her mouth.)

FRANK: And then we saw the blood. A lot of blood and screaming and no one was even watching the movie anymore. They were all looking at her. They were all staring at her with her bloody arms and her crazy eyes because . . .

ANGIE: Because she was the prettiest girl in the room.

RADIUM GIRLS
Dolores Whiskeyman
Man & Woman

Scene: Orange, New Jersey, 1918.

Grace (sixteen to seventeen), a top-notch dial painter, and Tom (sixteen to eighteen), her hardworking boyfriend.

Grace works in a factory painting radium onto watch dials. As she and Tom dream about their future together, the lethal substance is already at work in her body, sealing her tragic fate.

TOM: So why do you wanna quit? I thought ya liked it up there.

GRACE: Been there four years.

TOM: So?

GRACE: Got to the point I dream about watch dials. Trays and trays of watch dials goin' by . . . all those little numbers glowin' in the dark. And at the end of the day, my fingers are so cramped and my back just aches so bad . . . use to be it stopped hurting once I got home, but now, it's all the time. I know I'm lucky to have what I do — I guess I shouldn't complain, should I?

TOM: Y'know what you need?

GRACE: A rich husband?

TOM: One of these.

(Tom leans in for a kiss — Grace stops him.)

GRACE: Tommy!

TOM: What?

GRACE: What if Papa walks in.

TOM: Maybe he'll learn something.

GRACE: Can't ya behave for even one minute?

TOM: I could. But ya wouldn't like it. Now where ya goin'?

GRACE: I got somethin' to show ya. Close yer eyes.

TOM: Yer mom's right, ya know. Ya better not quit till ya get something else. Ya never know how long it might be — and bein' outta work's no picnic. I been there. And I'm tellin' ya, Grace — there's nothin' like havin' a rock-solid position with a good pension to help ya sleep at night.

GRACE: Okay, now look.

(Tom looks.)

TOM: Wallpaper?

GRACE: What do ya think?

TOM: What's it for?

GRACE: Baby's room.

TOM: Baby's room! Ya won't kiss me and yer talkin' about babies?

GRACE: There's gonna be babies eventually.

TOM: Y'know Grace, most girls — they get married before they decorate the nursery.

GRACE: Plan ahead for once. Pick one.

TOM: They're both the same.

GRACE: No they're not. This one has big flowers, and that one has little flowers. So pick one.

TOM: This some kinda test?

GRACE: No. It's just wallpaper.

TOM: It is some kinda test.

GRACE: Pick one.

TOM: That one.

GRACE: Really?

TOM: The other one then.

GRACE: Which do you like, though?

TOM: They're both nice.

GRACE: This one is pretty, don't you think?

TOM: That one, then.

GRACE: But I want you to like it, too.

TOM: If you like it, I'll like it. Wallpaper is wallpaper.

GRACE: No it ain't. Ya gotta pick somethin' ya can stand to look at for 20 years.

TOM: Same way ya pick women?

GRACE: Keep it up. And you'll never get that kiss.

TOM: This one. This one, hands down.

GRACE: I like it, too. A nice neutral yellow goes with either a boy or a girl. And then when the baby's grown, ya use the room for other things.

TOM: Yeah? Like what?

GRACE: Like. A painting studio, maybe?

TOM: A painting studio maybe? Don't ya get enough of that at work?

GRACE: This is different. If ya have a nice sunny back room, ya could set up an easel and leave it there. I could do landscapes in watercolors or pastels — maybe portraits, in oil. I could paint yer picture if you like.

TOM: Why not? Paint a big picture of me and we'll hang it in the outhouse. All our friends will come round just to use the can, so's they can look at it.

GRACE: The way you talk sometimes.

TOM: Ya wanna paint pictures. Paint pictures. I ain't gonna stop ya.

GRACE: Ya say that now. But just wait until we're married. Ya'll come home some night all wore out — some Christmas maybe, when every customer on yer route's had three times the mail — and maybe some dog took after ya and some old lady kept ya waiting on the stoop tellin' ya all about her grandchildren — 'cause ya wouldn't have the heart to tell her ya can't talk — I know you. And so ya come home, all cranky and late besides, hungry — wantin' your dinner. And there I am, I got my easel set up in the kitchen, drop cloth on the floor, my paints all over the table — and yer dinner's nowhere in sight. What would ya say, then?

TOM: Better be a picture of me you're paintin'.

GRACE: Y'know what ya'd say? Where's my dinner! That's what ya'd say. Where's my dinner?

TOM: Well, sure. But I'd still admire the painting. Just like to look at it on a full stomach, is all. *(Beat.)* So how'd I do? Pick the right wallpaper?

GRACE: I don't know. Maybe I'll go look at stripes.

(He gets a kiss.)

TOM: Yer mouth still hurt?

GRACE: Little bit.

TOM: What did the dentist say?

GRACE: Oh. He's got to pull another tooth. In the back.

TOM: Well. What's a tooth?

ROMEO & JULIET II
Sandra Hosking
Man & Woman

Scene: Verona.

Romeo and Juliet, older and wiser.

The bloom is off the rose, as we can see in the following scene in which Romeo and Juliet carp and snipe like an old married couple.

JULIET: *(Calling offstage.)* Romeo! Romeo! Where art thou Romeo! Get your lily-white ass in here!

JULIET: *(Sigh.)* Aye me.

ROMEO: *(Entering.)* What Juliet?

JULIET: What? What do you think? Am I not slaving here? Do you not see that I am with child? Your child?

ROMEO: What? No 'good eve' for your true love Romeo.

JULIET: Ha! Fetch me the plates from the shelf.

ROMEO: The babes are abed?

JULIET: Aye they are. Fed, washed, and safely tucked in by their mother. Fat cow that she is. *(He hands her two plates.)* I need another.

ROMEO: Who is the third party at my table. I pray 'tis not your father.

JULIET: Why not my father?

ROMEO: Know you not how he needles me?

JULIET: I call it guiding.

ROMEO: Goading. He does not respect my work.

JULIET: What work is that?

ROMEO: I am a poet.

JULIET: A fop. You dream of poetry. The proof is in the sheaf.

ROMEO: *(Sarcastic.)* You are the flower of cordiality. Prithee put my mind at ease, dear wife.

JULIET: Relax. My father is safe within the walls of his own courtyard. Though I should invite him to supper to spite you. No, rest easy, Love. It is Friar Lawrence who comes.

ROMEO: Aah. The good friar. I should lock up the wine then. Last time he drank himself into a river.

JULIET: Where have you been today? Did you speak to the silversmith as Papa suggested?

ROMEO: I did begin my journey there, but was captured by a glorious column of trees all aglow with white blossoms. Their petals fell to the ground as snow. It reminded me of our wedding, Mo Cheri. I settled in to watch the scene for but a moment, and my eyes closed as if under a spell.

JULIET: You tarried.

ROMEO: I was bewitched.

JULIET: You slept all day!

ROMEO: I was lost.

JULIET: You sloth! You snail! Sicilian slug! You are as slow as an old woman walking up a steep hill. All the world moves 'round her while she inches upward. Papa was right about you.

ROMEO: Popinjay.

JULIET: Clog.

ROMEO: Argh. Your voice is as thunder. I am no slug. And your father knows nothing of it.

JULIET: No work. No trade. No money. A dozen. A dozen — soon to be 13 — mouths to feed in this hovel. What shall I feed them? Dirt and grubs? Shall I dress the children of Romeo Montague in sackcloths? Where shall we live when you dream away our means? Romeo. Romeo. Your name brings laughter to the people in the town. Do you not hear what they say when we walk Verona's streets. "Look there," they say, "there go poor Romeo's urchins and his vericose wife. Make way for the monkey Montagues!"

ROMEO: There was a time when we cared not a whit about the words of others. We ignored their stares and whispers. Remember?

JULIET: I can only remember what I see before me. I'll endure it no longer, my husband.

ROMEO: What can you do to manage the beasts of the town?

JULIET: Money.

ROMEO: Money?

JULIET: I aim to tame the town with money.

ROMEO: Where comes this money?

JULIET: I shall work.

ROMEO: What?

JULIET: Are you deaf?

ROMEO: I am dumb. What shall be your trade?

JULIET: I shall bake bread and sell it in the square.

ROMEO: My wife, a common peddler?

JULIET: Better to be industrious than feeble minded. I'll not dwell in the kitchen while my husband wanders as a feckless fly.

ROMEO: Feckless?!

JULIET: I go to fetch water.

ROMEO: Let me help.

JULIET: No. Rest. It is your best occupation.

SCENE ANALYSIS FOR FUN AND PROFIT
Bob Jude Ferrante
Man & Woman

Scene: A dining room in a middle-class American home.

Dana (thirty-four), a disgruntled wife, and Frank (thirty to forty), her husband.

Frank's in big trouble, as the following scene reveals.

> *A dining room in a middle-class American home. Dana, thirty-four, sits at the dining table. On the table is the clear evidence of a very ornate meal, carefully and lovingly prepared. Candles are lit and nearly burnt down to the bottom; a bottle of wine in an ice bucket is opened; Dana sips from a glass. It becomes rapidly evident that she is quite drunk. Enter Frank, hurriedly, throwing his coat and briefcase onto a chair. The room is bathed in a cool blue light.*

FRANK: Breathless greeting.
DANA: Weak greeting in reply.
FRANK: Sincere-sounding apology for lateness.
DANA: Comment about husband not at least calling.
FRANK: Apology about meeting which ran way over and no access to telephones.
DANA: Reminder that Frank has cellphone.
FRANK: Observation that in general it is rude to use a cellphone in a meeting.
DANA: Counter-observation that it is rude not to call when you are late.
FRANK: Commentary about partner's ability to judge rudeness.
DANA: Inquiry about meaning.
FRANK: Refusal to comment further.
DANA: Refusal to continue until meaning is made clear.
FRANK: Apparent surrender with an angry mention of party last week where she got drunk and vomited on neighbor's carpet.

DANA: Total dismissal of husband's version of the story, claiming a stomach virus as the actual culprit.

FRANK: Statement that one should not have eight vodka tonics when one has a stomach virus.

DANA: Admission that drinking might be due to a valid relationship reason, e.g., that he is not paying enough sexual attention to her.

FRANK: Very macho and arrogant reply.

(The light rapidly changes to natural room light.)

DANA: What the fuck is that supposed to mean?

FRANK: Well, how are we supposed to have normal sexual relations if you're drunk every night when I get home?

DANA: That's the point! I never know when you are going to get home. I mean, you said you'd be home at seven-thirty and here it is, ten-thirty. You ruin every night, just like you ruined dinner tonight!

FRANK: You didn't tell me you were cooking a goddamned feast!

DANA: You're right. I didn't.

(Dana sits. The light changes back to blue.)

DANA: Invitation to sit down and finish the dinner.

FRANK: Statement that he'd already grabbed something on the way home.

DANA: Entreaty to at least taste the stew, made from a new recipe acquired from a prominent women's magazine.

FRANK: Snide reference to testing using laboratory animals.

DANA: Comparison of husband's sexual member to that of an albino lab rat.

(The light changes back to normal room light.)

FRANK: Jesus Christ! I can't believe you said that!

DANA: Well you insulted my cooking.

FRANK: Putting down cooking is one thing. I didn't get personally insulting.

DANA: The whole way you treat me is personally insulting.

FRANK: Well if you got out more and maybe got a job or something, maybe I would respect you more.

DANA: Why is this about me? You're the one who doesn't know the first thing about making a woman happy! You treat me like a piece of dirt. I'm the last thing you think about.

(Frank approaches Dana and puts a hand on her shoulder.)

DANA: Don't touch me!

FRANK: I'm sorry! I thought your complaint was I don't touch you. I was just trying to be responsive.

DANA: You're just trying to calm me down.

FRANK: No! Honestly! I'm really sorry and I want things to work between us.
 (Beat.)

 DANA: Really?
 (The light changes back to blue.)

FRANK: Assurance of sincerity.

DANA: Pained statement that she was starting to lose hope.

FRANK: Question about what he can do to prove he means what he says.

DANA: Request for a night out.

FRANK: Pause. Then agreement.

DANA: More specific request: A night out at a very, very exclusive four-star restaurant.

FRANK: Longer pause, then a reference to some financial pressures that have surfaced lately making this unlikely.

DANA: Question about what he means, and a statement that he took a job with more hours so they could have enough money to be spontaneous.

FRANK: Reference to their recent vacation in Aruba as an example of something spontaneous.
 (Dana goes over to the secretary desk and opens it, then takes out a sheet of paper.)

DANA: Retort that Frank spent the entire vacation working on his new laptop.

FRANK: Reply that all Dana wanted to do was visit the swim-up bar.
 (Dana waves the piece of paper in Frank's face.)

DANA: Question of a line item stating there was a jewelry store purchase on the credit card bill.

FRANK: Casual reply that it must be an erroneous charge.

DANA: Slightly more acid-toned statement that the credit card company has a signed slip from him for the charge.

FRANK: Question about meaning: Is she saying Frank is buying jewelry for himself and not spending enough money on Dana?

DANA: Correction. Is Frank buying jewelry for someone else.

FRANK: Request for more clear statement. Is Dana implying Frank is having an affair or something?

DANA: Inquiry as to what other cause the mysterious charge could have had.

FRANK: Pretense at being totally befuddled.

DANA: Overtly palliative answer with a subtext of frustration and anger.

FRANK: Question about tone in voice.

DANA: Question about *what* tone in voice?

FRANK: Complete uncertainty as to how to reply.

DANA: Assertion that everything is probably OK then.

FRANK: A pause. *(Pause.)* Tentative question if that's actually the case.

(The light changes back to normal.)

DANA: No, you stupid motherfucker! I was just testing to see if you'd lie to me, even after you were caught like a rat in a trap!

FRANK: All you have to do is check it again. I'm telling you, I've been really careful not to put too many things on the charge cards.

DANA: Right. Careful is the critical word, as in careful to hide what's going on! I've also checked our ATM withdrawals, which have doubled in the past four months! I bounced a check to Piggly Wiggly yesterday.

FRANK: I swear to you, I'm not having an affair with Sara.

DANA: Who said Sara?

FRANK: Or anyone. Isn't that what you're saying?

DANA: I never said Sara.

FRANK: It had to be Sara! It was written all over this conversation.

DANA: Well, now it's written all over, you could have Sara type the fucking thing up for you! Bastard!

FRANK: I'm trying to say, I'm not having —

DANA: I can't believe this! It's true! I was half hoping it was a delusion! But it's true!

FRANK: Dana, be reasonable here.

DANA: Oh. Sure.

(Dana picks up the near empty bottle of wine and pours it over Frank's head.)

FRANK: Please, Dana. This is a good suit!

DANA: I know. I picked it out for you, you fashion *excuse.*

(She picks up a plate and throws it at his feet.)

These are good shoes, too!

FRANK: Christ! I can't take this any more. I've got to get out of here!

DANA: Oh no, don't go. I'm not done decorating you yet!

(Frank runs out.)

DANA: Great! Get the hell out of here! Asshole!

(Beat. Then a man comes out from under the dining room table. The light turns blue again.)

MAN: Expression of relief that husband is gone.

DANA: Complete agreement.

MAN: Complaint about a stress pain in right knee from hiding under the table.

DANA: Suggestion that after dinner, some therapeutic activity for the knee are possible.

MAN: Reply that there are other areas with problems as well.

DANA: Agreement, and addendum that a sex therapist could help with that.

(The lights change back to normal.)

MAN: I meant I was in the mood, not that I had those kinds of problems!

DANA: Well if you thought about my needs for once, instead of the needs of your little pee pee, maybe —

MAN: Little pee pee? That's it, bitch! I'm leaving!

(Man walks out and slams the door. Silence. The lights turn blue.)

DANA: Final, amusing statement prior to blackout.

(Blackout.)

SIDE MAN
Warren Leight
Man & Woman

Scene: New York City, 1950s.

Terry (twenties), a passionate young mother-to-be, and Gene (twenty to thirty), her husband, a jazz musician.

With the advent of Elvis Presley, times are tough for jazz sidemen like Gene. Here, pregnant Terry hands her out-of-work husband a severe ultimatum.

TERRY: *(To Gene.)* You lied to me. When Jonesy was arrested the first time, it wasn't disorderly conduct, was it? It was for junk, wasn't it?

GENE: I guess — I mean, he's not really a junkie junkie. More of an addict. He never misses a gig.

TERRY: He told me he doesn't have any gigs.

GENE: It's a little slow right now. No one works in September — the Jewish holidays.

TERRY: Patsy says it's all over. Elvis. TV. L.A. Jazz is —

GENE: Patsy is just pissed off because she can't get Al or Bernie or Ziggy to quit so she had to go back to Stu who spends his day touching people's feet. Is that what you want me to do?

TERRY: That's the same Bernie who got credit for your solos, isn't it?

GENE: Most likely. So *what.*

TERRY: Why don't you send out those scripts you and Ziggy wrote?

GENE: They're not ready.

TERRY: Do you want me to help?

GENE: Honey, you can barely speak English; no one understands a word you say. How the hell are you going to help with the scripts?

TERRY: Fuck you.

GENE: What? Oh don't get upset. I'm just saying. Ziggy and I went to college. We know what we're doing. As soon as those scripts are ready — they're going out.

TERRY: Do you have a gig for tonight?

GENE: Not yet.

TERRY AND GENE: Huh.

GENE: It happens. What's the big deal.

TERRY: It's Saturday night.

GENE: The Jewish holidays. No one's working.

TERRY: But it's Saturday night.

GENE: Terry, I've got my twenty weeks in, I subbed at the Copa twice last week, what's so goddamn important about Saturday night. Jesus — a gig is a gig.

TERRY: You said if you ever weren't booked for a Saturday night, you'd quit the business.

GENE: Oh, come on. I never said that.

(She stares at him in disbelief, then anger.)

TERRY: You lying motherfucker —

GENE: Terry —

(She walks away from him.)

TERRY: You lying motherfucker —

(Terry doesn't see Gene as he moves toward her.)

GENE: Terry, get a hold of your —

(He is suddenly next to her. She bats him away.)

TERRY: Get your hands off me, Dominic —

GENE: I'm Gene.

TERRY: I don't care who you are. All of you. Stay away. I can't take this bullshit. All of you lie. All of you fucking lie.

GENE: STOP IT. Stop it.

(She snaps back to reality. Calms a bit.)

TERRY: What time is it?

GENE: Nine.

TERRY: You have until midnight. If that phone doesn't ring, and you stay in the business, I'll fuckin' kill you. And I'll kill the baby.

(She takes her drink and walks past Gene to the bedroom as Clifford sits.)

TERRY: I swear to God, I'll kill you both.

(She slams the bedroom door behind her.)

SYNCOPATION
Allan Knee
Man & Woman

Scene: New York City, 1911.

Henry (thirties) and Anna (twenty to thirty), dance partners on the verge of a breakup.

Henry and Anna have battled their mutual attraction for quite some time, which is difficult as they're constantly in each other's arms. When Anna grows distant, Henry makes inquiries, which produce unhappy results.

HENRY: Anna!

ANNA: What is it now?

HENRY: I saw you.

ANNA: You're always seeing me. I look up and there you are. There's no surprise, Henry.

HENRY: I saw you at the railway station.

ANNA: I make no secret about going there.

HENRY: Who's the tall woman you're always talking to?

ANNA: Mildred.

HENRY: I don't like her.

ANNA: You don't know her. You don't like things you don't know, Henry. It's obvious. She's a remarkable woman. She fights for her beliefs. She's been in street brawls. She's been imprisoned twice. She has three daughters — and she raises them by herself.

HENRY: She looks angry.

ANNA: A lot of women are.

HENRY: Are you?

ANNA: At times I'm furious.

HENRY: *(Explodes.)* Well, I could smash walls in!
Who's the man?

ANNA: What man?

HENRY: The one who wears a cape.

ANNA: Someone I've met at the railway station.

HENRY: What's his name?

ANNA: His name is DeAngelos.

HENRY: What's he do?

ANNA: Things. Reads. Writes. He gives talks.

HENRY: Talks?

ANNA: On economic equality. On politics.

HENRY: He looks like someone out of a penny thriller.

ANNA: This man has been written up in newspapers. He's distinguished. And very important.

HENRY: What does he want from you?

ANNA: Nothing.

HENRY: I think he wants something.

ANNA: I'm going home.

HENRY: We should compete next week. I've written out a schedule. Five days —

ANNA: I can't do all that, Henry.

HENRY: We've got to keep moving on.

ANNA: I am!

HENRY: *(Inner turmoil mounting.)* What do you want from this man?

ANNA: He opens my mind. He makes me think. He excites me.

HENRY: What about this schedule? At least agree to some of the competition.

ANNA: I'll think about it.

HENRY: I saw you whisper in his ear. I saw you hold his arm.

ANNA: I frequently hold men's arms.

HENRY: What about my arm?

ANNA: We should stop this conversation now —

HENRY: At least agree to Saturday night —

ANNA: I'm busy.

HENRY: But Saturday night is our night.

ANNA: *Was* our night, Henry.

HENRY: *(After a beat.)* I followed you last Saturday. You went to a hotel with this man.

ANNA: This has got to stop!

HENRY: I waited five hours for you. I waited, Anna. I waited and waited —

ANNA: What for?

HENRY: To see you. To see that you were all right. He's using you.

ANNA: He took me to dinner. And then we sat and talked. He told me stories — marvelous stories —

HENRY: Stop lying to me! Lie to the rest of the world, but not to me! Please, not to me! Tell *me* the truth! At least give me that!

ANNA: What do you want to know? All the sadness that's in me? All the longings? The dreams? The disappointments? The rages? . . . You want to see the wild woman that's in me? The little girl that's in me? You want to know if I love this man?

HENRY: Do you?

ANNA: With all my heart and soul. Like I've never loved anybody or anything in my life. I live to see him — to touch him. There's nothing I wouldn't do for him. No place I wouldn't go with him. Is that enough?

HENRY: What about Mr. Parva?

ANNA: Mr. Parva doesn't exist for me anymore. Mr. Angelos and I are going away together.

HENRY: Going away?

ANNA: He wants to marry me.

HENRY: He's proposed?

ANNA: Yes.

HENRY: When are you going?

ANNA: Soon.

HENRY: And what about us?

ANNA: This is painful, Henry.

HENRY: Are we over?

ANNA: I don't know.

HENRY: You'll continue to dance with me?

ANNA: I haven't asked him.

HENRY: You have to ask him? I would have thought you'd have your own opinion on this.

ANNA: Do you know what it's like to have a fantasy come to life? To love someone who once seemed so beyond you? Do you understand that?

HENRY: Yes.

ANNA: He's magnificent.

HENRY: You'll be happy with him?

ANNA: I really don't think you understand. You're a small man. I'm sorry if that hurts you. I don't mean to hurt you. I found someone who makes me feel complete. When he touches me — I come to life. I'm not going to give that up, Henry. Not for you — not for anyone.

HENRY: I wouldn't give that up. It's something I'd like to do. Make a woman feel complete.

ANNA: You live in this tiny little room that reeks of dust — and ghosts.

HENRY: Did our dancing mean anything to you?

ANNA: . . . Yes.

HENRY: But not very much.

ANNA: Sometimes it seemed to go very deep.

HENRY: I think it was always just a diversion. I think you've been waiting for this caped man — this talker — all your life.

ANNA: Good-bye, Henry.

THE THREE BIG LOVES OF CHRISTOPHER J. TOMASKI

Patrick Gabridge
Man & Woman

Scene: The outdoor courtyard of an old house in a small town.

Chris (late twenties) a man mourning the suicide death of his sister and Mona (fifties) his mother.

Following his sister's death, Chris visits home where he is confronted by his lonely mother who begs him to spend more time with her.

MONA: Oh, my God!

CHRIS: Mom.

MONA: Oh, God, please save my son. How long ago did you do it? Sit down, lower the pressure. It looks like you missed the vein. Oh, please, please. They warned me. It's almost contagious, suicide. Everyone in town is watching their kids. Everyone but me.

CHRIS: Mom, stop.

MONA: We'll get you to a doctor, don't worry. Wiesman. He can keep quiet. Don't die on me, Chris. You are my rock, you held us all together.

CHRIS: Mom, it's just a scratch. It's nothing.

MONA: What are you saying?

CHRIS: It was an accident.

MONA: You didn't do this to yourself?

CHRIS: Give me a break.

MONA: I know it's been a hard time for you.

CHRIS: I am not sending out a "cry for help."

MONA: You're sure?

CHRIS: You have nothing to worry about.

MONA: You're the one thing in my life that's worked out.

CHRIS: Untrue. The travel agency is booming.

MONA: It's of no consequence. Come here.

(She opens her arms for a hug. It lasts a long time, longer than he's comfortable with. Finally he breaks off.)

MONA: Thank you.

CHRIS: Anytime.

MONA: Please don't go.

CHRIS: I haven't decided.

MONA: You know how it is here. I'm walled off. I show them the pictures, but they still blame me. They won't drive me out of business, because I'm cheap. The bloodsuckers can't resist a bargain. But I'm isolated. I'm not asking you to stay forever. But I . . . I get all cooped up in that house, that dinky little house with your father there, always there. If I have someone to talk to, someone who understands . . . I really don't think I'm asking too much. At least consider it.

CHRIS: I will. I am. But my job —

MONA: Can be replaced. Can't you program computers out here? There must be a thousand places. You're young. I'm not asking you to commit your whole life, nothing like that. Very short term. In the long view, it's a drop, a speck of your time. For me, it would be a lifesaver.

CHRIS: And there's Lisa.

MONA: Lisa is a very nice young woman. I think she's very special. You two have been dating long enough to really know each other. But when someone loves you, they stick by you, no matter what. They don't issue ultimatums. They don't just walk out of your life. To leave, even to threaten, shows a complete lack of understanding and consideration. I don't want to seem harsh, but to leave, like that, would be evil.

CHRIS: She is not evil; she's looking out for me. She thinks . . . she sees what's going on around here, and she wants to protect me. She just doesn't know how. What she means to me, I can't —

MONA: She's had you to herself for two years and now she doesn't want to share you even for a short while, even when the need is dire.

CHRIS: You don't understand her at all.

MONA: I'm telling you what I see. Look, I need time with my son. I'll confess, I may even be a little desperate, but desperation is not a crime. You've been gone so long, you've missed so much of this whole ordeal.

CHRIS: I know. I'm sorry.

MONA: Don't be. It was not pleasant. It is not pleasant now. But it would be bearable if you were here.

CHRIS: I said I'd think about it.

MONA: You do that. Think about what's important. About responsibilities and obligations. Please.

TOUCH

Toni Press-Coffman

2 Men, 1 Woman

Scene: Here and now.

Kyle (thirties) a man mourning for his murdered wife; Serena (twenties) his wife's sister; and Bennie (thirties) his best friend.

When Kyle discovers that Bennie and Serena have begun a relationship, he overreacts, leading to the unsavory revelation that he has been visiting a prostitute since his wife's death. What follows is an angry confrontation that finally makes way for healing.

SERENA: Oh my God. *(Bennie holds her close.)*
BENNIE: Jesus Christ, Kyle.
KYLE: Jesus Christ what? Jesus Christ I caught you?
BENNIE: Caught me? No, you didn't catch me, I'm not a kindergarten kid.
  (Pause. Kyle moves around the room, agitated.)
SERENA: Hello, Kyle.
KYLE: I wish you'd get dressed.
SERENA: That's a good idea.
  (Kyle looks away as Serena puts on or buttons her blouse. She smoothes her hair.)
SERENA: I'm dressed.
KYLE: You're Zoe's sister.
SERENA: And here I thought you'd forgotten.
  (Kyle turns to her.)
KYLE: No. *(Pause.)* What is this?
SERENA: What does it look like?
KYLE: It looks like my best friend is fucking my dead wife's sister and hiding it from me.
SERENA: That's what it is.
KYLE: How long have you two been — um —
SERENA: Together?

KYLE: Yes.

SERENA: Since New Year's Eve.

KYLE: *(To Bennie.)* You've been fucking Zoe's sister since New Year's Eve?

BENNIE: Kyle, watch your mouth.

SERENA: No. *(To Kyle.)* That's right. We've been fucking since December 31. We drank champagne, we listened to John Klemmer. We made love on your sofa. Then we —

KYLE: I get the picture.

SERENA: *(Continuing.)* — took a couple of breaths, and then we made love on your living room floor.

(Kyle bangs his fist against a piece of furniture — maybe something falls off and breaks.)

KYLE: Enough.

BENNIE: *(Gesturing to Serena to shush.)* Sit down, Kyle.

KYLE: No.

BENNIE: Sit down, I'll get you a beer or something.

KYLE: I don't want to sit down. I don't want a beer. I want an explanation.

BENNIE: You want an explanation?

KYLE: I gave you an explanation.

BENNIE: You're comparing my feeling for Serena with your going to a whore?

SERENA: What?

KYLE: *(Overlap.)* No, I couldn't be doing that because I don't know anything about your feeling for Serena.

SERENA: You went to a prostitute?

KYLE: Not went. Still.

SERENA: How often?

KYLE: Often.

SERENA: Is that in honor of Zoe's memory, Kyle?

BENNIE: Shh. Serena.

KYLE: *(Overlap.)* Yes. It is.

SERENA: How respectful.

KYLE: *(Now he's really furious.)* Are you saying I don't respect Zoe? How can you say — how can you think — I would do anything disrespectful of Zoe?

SERENA: Tell me, Kyle. How is going to a whore respecting Zoe?

BENNIE: Come on, Serena.

(During the next speech, Kyle closes his eyes and starts to breathe.)

SERENA: That one's too hard? Then tell me something else. How is banishing her family from your life respecting her, Kyle? You think she's up in heaven smiling down at you while you ignore her mother and her father, while you refuse to see Trevor and me, while you pretend none of us has any pain or ever loved you, and while you instead take your grief to a prostitute and pay her to alleviate it?

BENNIE: Sweetheart —

SERENA: Alleviate it for — how long does it take, Kyle? Ten minutes? Five? Yes, I'm certain Zoe's spirit is out there thrilled, she's not just smiling down on you, I'm sure she's not just smiling —

BENNIE: Stop, Serena.

SERENA: No, I'm certain she's grinning broadly, grinning from ear to ear.

BENNIE: Shut up.

SERENA: Yes, she's delighted — don't maintain contact with anyone who loved me, dearest. No. Find a woman for hire and pay her twenty-five bucks to let you stick it in.

BENNIE: God.

(Silence. Serena moves to Kyle and speaks quietly, but intensely.)

SERENA: I don't know where the hell you are, but open your eyes and come back here because I am not going to allow you to ignore me anymore.

(Kyle opens his eyes. He and Serena stand very close to one another, looking at each other directly, intensely. A couple beats.)

KYLE: Zoe was smiling when we found her.

(Serena turns to Bennie, surprised.)

BENNIE: She was.

(Serena looks back to Kyle.)

KYLE: That's first. You should know that. *(Pause.)* Second. It costs more than twenty-five dollars.

(Serena tries to stop herself, but she laughs.)

BENNIE: *(Also laughing.)* No cheap whore for Kyle.

KYLE: She's worth it. She's a nice woman. *(Pause, then to Bennie.)* You didn't want me to know.

BENNIE: You didn't want to know.

KYLE: You called Serena sweetheart.

BENNIE: Yeah.

(Long pause.)

KYLE: The police caught them. The men who killed Zoe.

BENNIE: What? When?

SERENA: Definitely?

KYLE: Yes.

> *(Serena moves to Kyle and puts her arms around him. They hold each other hard. A telephone ringing can be heard faintly.)*

KYLE: Yes. Definitely.

THE TRESTLE AT POPE LICK CREEK

Naomi Wallace

Man & Woman

Scene: A town outside an American city, 1936.

Pace (seventeen) a young woman filled with a dark passion for living, and Dalton (fifteen to sixteen) a young man coming of age.

Here, Pace and Dalton meet beneath the railroad trestle where Brett, Pace's boyfriend, was killed a year before in a terrible accident. Dalton is fascinated with Pace despite himself as the following scene reveals.

Pace and Dalton run to meet under the trestle at Pope Lick Creek. Pace gets there ahead of Dalton. They have been running and are both out of breath.

DALTON: You had a head start!

PACE: Nah. You haven't got any lungs in that puny chest of yours. Listen to you rattle.

DALTON: I'm not rattlin'.

PACE: Yeah you are. What've you got in there? A handful of nails.

DALTON: Twisted my ankle.

PACE: Yeah, yeah.

DALTON: So this is it, huh?

(They look up above them.)

PACE: Yep.

DALTON: It's not that high up.

PACE: Almost a hundred feet. From the creek up.

DALTON: Some creek. There's no water: it's dry.

PACE: Don't care; can't swim anyway. What time is it?

DALTON: Coming up to seven.

PACE: Exact time.

DALTON: *(Guessing.)* Six forty-one.

PACE: She comes through at seven ten. Sometimes seven twelve. Sometimes she'll come on at seven nine for ten days straight and then bang, she's off three minutes. She's never exact; you can't trust her. That's what I like.

DALTON: How many times have you done it?

PACE: Twice. Once with Jeff Farley. Once alone.

DALTON: You're lyin'. Jeff Farley never ran it.

PACE: Nope. Never did. Tied his shoes on real tight, took two deep breaths, said "I'm ready when you are." And then he heard that whistle. Aren't a lot of people can hear that whistle.

DALTON: So you didn't do it twice.

PACE: I would of but he turned tail and ran.

DALTON: So how many times then? Just once?

PACE: Once. And that's once more than you.

DALTON: Yeah. Who was witness?

PACE: No one here to see me.

DALTON: You're lying.

PACE: Whatever you say.

DALTON: Did you run it or not?

PACE: Sure. Once.

DALTON: How come I don't believe you?

PACE: Me and you, we'll have witnesses. Philip, Lester and Laura Sutton will be here at seven-o-five.

DALTON: No. No way. You said just you and me as witness.

PACE: If you get scared and run, who's to say you won't lie and say I chickened too?

DALTON: You said you and me.

PACE: It'll be just you and me. Up there. Down here in the creek bed we'll have the three stooges watching us. Keeping tabs. Taking notes. And you can be sure they'll check our pants when we're done and see who's shit.

DALTON: You know. You don't talk like a girl. Should.

PACE: *(Meaning it.)* Thanks.

DALTON: But you look like one. So I guess you are.

PACE: Want me to prove it?

DALTON: No.

PACE: How old are you?

DALTON: Sixteen. In a couple of months.

PACE: *(Nears him.)* Well, well. Almost a man. *(Pushes him backwards, but not too hard.)* Listen to me, Dalton Chance, two years my junior, and shut up. Here's what we're going to do.

DALTON: Just spell it out for me. Once and clear.

PACE: Okay. She's pulling eight cars at seventy tons apiece at eighty-five. Not a big one, as far as they go. But big enough. The engine herself's one hundred and fifty-three tons. And not cotton, kid. Just cold, lip smackin' steel. Imagine a kiss like that. Just imagine it.

DALTON: How do you know what the train weighs?

PACE: I looked her up. The year, the weight, the speed.

DALTON: So you can read.

PACE: Yeah, well. You and her are coming from opposite sides, right. You've got to time it exact 'cause you need to make it across before she hits the trestle. It's like playin' chicken with a car, only she's bigger and you're not a car. The kick is once you get half way across, don't turn back and try to out-run her. You lose time like that. Just face her and go.

DALTON: So what if you know it's too close? You go for the side, right?

PACE: There's no side.

DALTON: Yes there is.

PACE: There's no side. Look at it.

DALTON: There's a side.

PACE: What's the matter with you? Look at the tracks. Look at them. There are no sides.

DALTON: So what do you do if you can't make it across before she starts over?

PACE: You make the cross. That's all there is to it.

DALTON: But what if you can't?

PACE: Remember Brett Weaver?

DALTON: That's different. He was drunk.

PACE: He was not.

DALTON: Yes he was. He was drunk.

PACE: Say that again and I'll punch you.

DALTON: The papers said he was drunk.

PACE: Brett wasn't drunk. He was just slow.

DALTON: Slow? He was on the track team.

PACE: That night he was slow.

DALTON: How do you know?

PACE: I just know.

DALTON: Well. I've had a look like I told you I would and I've decided: I'm not crossing.

PACE: I knew it. I knew it.

DALTON: Only a drunk or an idiot'd play that game. Not me.

PACE: You got the heart of a rabbit. A dead rabbit. And now you owe me a buck.

DALTON: No way. I never said for certain. I said maybe. And you said it was safe. You didn't say anything about there being no safety sides. You said it was a piece of cake.

PACE: It is a piece of cake. If you time it right.

DALTON: Forget it.

PACE: You're breaking the deal. Pay me a buck right now or else.

DALTON: I said no.

PACE: *(Calmly pulls a switch blade.)* Then I'll hurt you.

DALTON: Put that away. You're warped. That's what everyone says at school: Pace Creagan is warped.

PACE: Then why'd you come up here with me? I'm not even your friend.

DALTON: No. You're not my friend. My friends don't pull knives.

PACE: You were starting to like me, though. I could tell. You said you'd run it with me.

DALTON: I said I might. I thought it could be fun. Warped people can be fun sometimes.

PACE: If you back down everyone will know.

DALTON: I don't care. I don't have a fan club.

PACE: Mary Ellen Berry is coming as witness too.

DALTON: No she's not.

PACE: I asked her to. And she knows you've got a fancy for her.

DALTON: Big deal. I asked her out. She turned me down. End of story.

PACE: She says you're too short.

DALTON: I'm too short.

PACE: I don't think she was talking height.

DALTON: I'm leaving.

PACE: Hey. I told her to give you a chance. She likes me. She listens to me. I told her you were going to cross the trestle with me. She said "oh." You know, like she was thinking things.

DALTON: What things?

PACE: You know. The way girls think things. One, two, three, about face.

Change of season. Oh. She said "oh" like she was about to change her mind.

DALTON: Mary Ellen's popular. Why would she listen to you.

PACE: *(Shrugs.)* I once told her to take off her clothes and she did.

DALTON: And what does that mean?

PACE: It means I can run faster than she can so she does what I tell her to do. And she'll be here tonight. She's coming to watch us cross.

DALTON: You had a look at her? Naked? What's she like?

PACE: I'd say she's on the menu. Front, back, and in reverse. You'd like her.

DALTON: How would you know what I like? You're not good-looking.

PACE: Yeah. But that's got nothing to do with trains.

DALTON: So how close were you that time you crossed?

PACE: I'd say I had 'bout eight seconds leeway.

DALTON: Eight seconds. Sure.

PACE: A kid could do it. Look. We won't do it tonight, okay. We'll work up to it. Tonight we'll just watch her pass. Take her measure. Check her steam. Make sure we got it down. Then when we're ready, we'll run her. It'll be a snap.

DALTON: A snap. What if you trip?

PACE: Brett tripped.

DALTON: He was messed up. Even if he wasn't drunk. He used to hit himself in the face just for the fun of it. Brett was mental. He'd hit his own nose until it bled.

PACE: Brett wasn't mental.

DALTON: I saw Brett hit himself. I saw him do it.

PACE: It's none of your business.

DALTON: You were his girl.

PACE: We were friends. I never kissed him. And you're gonna run the trestle. One of these days.

DALTON: How come?

PACE: 'Cause if you don't your life will turn out just like you think it will: quick, dirty and cold.

DALTON: Hey, I might go to college when I graduate.

PACE: You're not going to college. None of us are going to college.

DALTON: I got the grades for it. That's what Mr. Pearson says.

PACE: And who's gonna pay for it? Look at your shoes.

DALTON: Huh?

PACE: Your shoes. If your Mom's putting you in shoes like that then you aren't going to college. *(Beat.)* Come on. Let's go up and watch.

DALTON: If I can't go to college, I'll just leave.

PACE: Some things should stay in one place, Dalton Chance. You're probably one of them.

THE UN-XMAS STORY

Jeff Goode

Man & Woman

Scene: A stable outside an inn in Bethlehem, about 2000 years ago.

Mary (eighteen to twenty) an exhausted and crabby new mother, and Joseph (twenties) her husband.

Joseph and Mary have been sent to the stables for lack of room at the inn. (Sound familiar?) Here, the new parents bicker over their accommodations and the questionable paternity of their infant son.

MARY: No room at the inn, my ass!

JOSEPH: Honey, calm down.

MARY: You saw that guy they let in right after us.

JOSEPH: Maybe he wanted a single.

MARY: A single? You think I wouldn't take a single? I wouldn't rather squeeze into a single than sleep out in the fucking barn?!

JOSEPH: Honey, lower your voice.

MARY: "Sorry, no vacancies. But the barn's available. We also have a lovely pig sty opening up in a few minutes, if you can wait."

JOSEPH: They didn't offer us the pig sty.

MARY: No, because that's extra. The in-room mud bath, you pay extra for that. I'm telling you, this isn't a "no room" thing, it's a "no money" thing. This wouldn't happen if you'd got that nice carpenter job like I told you.

JOSEPH: They weren't hiring.

MARY: They *were* hiring, you just took too long getting down there and they went with someone else.

JOSEPH: They wanted experience.

MARY: They wanted punctuality is what they wanted.

JOSEPH: Okay, this is not my fault.

MARY: I don't see anybody else sleeping in a barn because they couldn't get a job. Oh, except for me.

JOSEPH: Did you ever think that maybe they have rules at the inn about letting two people share a single together when they're not married? Did you ever think of that?

MARY: And whose fault is that, Mr. Cold Feet? Mr. I-don't-know-if-I'm-ready-for-this. Mr. It's-All-Happening-So-Fast-I-Think-We-Both-Need-Time-To-Think.

JOSEPH: You are unbelievable.

MARY: You didn't even check in under your own name, for God's sake. Mr. "Of Nazareth" and friend. What is that? I'm your friend?

JOSEPH: You're not my wife.

MARY: I *am* your wife. Eyes o' God, and don't you forget it.

JOSEPH: That is not my child.

MARY: Okay, we're not going to get into this again.

JOSEPH: Well, it's not!

MARY: I don't know if I'd go there if I were you, considering I see a lot of farming tools around here and you do have to sleep sometime.

JOSEPH: I wasn't going to bring it up.

MARY: You did bring it up.

JOSEPH: I wasn't going to, but you keep . . .

MARY: Watch it.

JOSEPH: Well, you do.

MARY: Careful.

JOSEPH: Sound like my mother.

MARY: What??

JOSEPH: You heard me.

MARY: You asshole!!

JOSEPH: See! You got a mouth like a fisherman. You get that from your mother.

MARY: You weren't complaining about my mouth when I was eight months pregnant and you still wanted to get biblical every single night.

JOSEPH: *(Covering his ears.)* Okay, I don't want to hear this. La la la la . . .

MARY: You're going to hear it!

JOSEPH: La la la la . . .

MARY: You don't think I have enough to worry about being eight months pregnant and my boyfriend can't afford a ring, so he wants to hold off on the wedding and it makes me look like the town whore? Oh my God, the baby! The baby!

JOSEPH: What?

MARY: Where's the baby?

JOSEPH: Oh shit.

MARY: Oh my God, you lost the baby again?

JOSEPH: He's around here somewhere.

MARY: He's up at the inn. You left him on the counter.

JOSEPH: I don't think so.

MARY: Go back and get him!

JOSEPH: Okay!

MARY: Go get my baby!!

JOSEPH: All right!

(He exits. She watches him outside.)

MARY: What are you doing?

JOSEPH: (Offstage.) He's right here with the luggage. He's fine.

(Joseph re-enters with a baby wrapped in swaddling clothes.)

MARY: He's not fine. You left him outside with the luggage. My God!

JOSEPH: He was on top.

MARY: (Taking the baby.) Oh you poor thing. You poor baby.

JOSEPH: I don't know what's the big deal. He's fine.

MARY: No thanks to you, you bastard.

JOSEPH: I don't think that's a word you want to be tossing around.

MARY: Oh! You are so lucky I have this baby.

JOSEPH: Yeah, he's brought me nothing but good fortune.

MARY: Okay, as soon as I find some place to set him down, you're a dead man.

JOSEPH: I'll get the rest of the bags.

(He goes out to get the rest of the luggage.)

MARY: I'm serious! When you get back in here, you're gonna get it.

(She looks around the barn for a place to put the baby. She doesn't find one. She starts to cry. Joseph comes back in with the rest of their bags.)

JOSEPH: Now what's wrong?

MARY: There's no place to put him.

JOSEPH: What do you mean? There's some straw.

MARY: He's not going to sleep on a pile of straw.

JOSEPH: *We're* going to sleep on a pile of straw.

MARY: He's a baby. He needs a crib.

JOSEPH: Fine. So lay him in the manger.

MARY: I can't put him a manger!

JOSEPH: Why not?

MARY: Because it's a trough! For animals! To eat from!

JOSEPH: Yeah, and it's also exactly the same construction as a crib. I know. I was almost a carpenter, remember?

MARY: And what if a cow wanders in here in the middle of the night looking for a snack?

JOSEPH: Oh, please.

MARY: And eats him?!

JOSEPH: I'll bolt the door.

MARY: He's not going in the manger.

JOSEPH: He's going in the manger.

MARY: He's not!

JOSEPH: *(Fed up.)* Fine. Give him to me. I'll hold him.

(Joseph takes the baby.)

MARY: What are you going to do?

JOSEPH: What's it look like? I'm going to stand here, and hold him, all night. While you get some sleep. While the two of you get some sleep, I'll be right here, holding the baby.

(He rocks the baby and sulks at the same time.)

MARY: Are you sure?

JOSEPH: You better get some rest. We've got a long day tomorrow.

(She watches him rocking the baby. It's very touching.)

MARY: You're going to make a wonderful father.

JOSEPH: I don't think you want to play that card right now.

MARY: Honey?

JOSEPH: I should hear sleeping right about now.

MARY: I know you don't like to talk about women's issues.

JOSEPH: *(Cringing.)* Oh, God, don't say "cramps."

MARY: But do you remember the time last spring when we went on that picnic out to Galilee? And we stayed out late and watched the sun set. And you told me stories about Moses and the Israelites. And parting the Red Sea.

JOSEPH: And you said sometimes I remind you of Moses.

MARY: And sometimes I remind you of the sea.

(Joseph blushes.)

MARY: Do you remember what we did that night?

(He blushes again and nods.)

MARY: Honey . . . That's how you make babies.

(Joseph is stunned.)

JOSEPH: No fucking way!

MARY: Uh huh.

JOSEPH: Oh God, I think I'm gonna be sick.

MARY: Honey?

JOSEPH: *You* did *that* with those *Romans*???

MARY: No! That's what I've been trying to tell you. Nothing happened. Okay, I flirted with some Romans. But that's it.

JOSEPH: That's it?

MARY: And I waved at one of them.

JOSEPH: And that's it?

MARY: And maybe I gave him one of these.

(She gives a coy smile and a wink.)

JOSEPH: You are such a slut.

MARY: Okay, I made a mistake, I admit it. I'm not perfect. I was mad at you and I wanted to make you jealous. But that's all the further it went. The things you and I did that weekend in Galilee . . .

(He blushes again.)

MARY: The parting of the seas. The turning staffs into snakes.

JOSEPH: The coveting my neighbor's ass?

MARY: The burning bush. The plague of "lick us." I've never done any of that with anyone else but you.

JOSEPH: Not even the Romans?

MARY: Not even the Romans.

JOSEPH: Not even the cute one?

MARY: Not even the cute one.

JOSEPH: That kept coming by your house? Because I saw him.

MARY: No one.

JOSEPH: Why didn't you tell me this before?

MARY: Because every time I so much as mention reproductive —

JOSEPH: Okay okay okay!

MARY: And because you were being such a jerk about the wedding, and I wanted to get back at you. And maybe I carried things a little too far. But, Honey, the baby? You're the father. He's your son.

JOSEPH: Really?

MARY: Uh huh.

(Joseph looks at the baby in his arms.)

MARY: Honey, why don't you put the baby in the manger and come to bed?

JOSEPH: Can I hold him a little longer?

MARY: There'll be time for that tomorrow.

(Mary takes the baby and puts it in the manger.)

JOSEPH: I don't know, I think one of us ought to stay up and watch for cows.

MARY: We'll both watch.

(They kneel next to the manger and watch over the baby.)

JOSEPH: Did I ever tell you about the time Moses wanted to keep his staff up in the air all night but his arms were getting tired, so Aaron had to help him out?

MARY: *(Smiles.)* A few times.

WAR OF THE WORLDS

Naomi Iizuka, conceived by Anne Bogart and
created by the SITI Company
Man & Woman

Scene: Here and now.

Orson Welles (forties) master filmmaker, and Leni Zadrov (thirties) an enigmatic actress.

Here, two great artists playfully spar as they discover essential truths about each other.

ZADROV: You. You know, you don't gain weight if nobody sees you eat.
WELLES: Is that right?
ZADROV: It's a known, scientific fact.
WELLES: I'm absolutely starving.
ZADROV: Still?
WELLES: Always. And you?
ZADROV: Starving.
WELLES: Where is this going exactly?
ZADROV: It's a digression.
WELLES: Is that what it is?
ZADROV: I like digressions, don't you? One mad little digression can make all
the difference in the world.
(A door closes. Darkness. Zadrov and Welles laugh in the darkness. Light returns, like a door opening. The feel of the world is different. Welles and Zadrov are not where we last saw them. A different angle. A different point in time.)
ZADROV: How did you do that?
WELLES: Like all good magic, the secret is ridiculously simple. You smile. I'm
being serious. I'm a great fan of yours, you know. I saw you in *Bird of Paradise.* I was seventeen. You were naked. You were underwater. You
were rescuing a wounded sailor. Do you always rescue wounded sailors?
ZADROV: Always. I can't help it. There's no logic. It's my character.

WELLES: Let's drink to character.

   (Lap dissolve. Welles snaps his fingers. Leni Zadrov awakes from a trance.)

ZADROV: Did you really hypnotize me?

WELLES: You were in a deep, deep sleep.

ZADROV: Why did you wake me?

WELLES: I was getting a little lonely. I like people to talk to me, you see.

ZADROV: What do you like them to say?

WELLES: That depends.

ZADROV: I'm afraid I never saw your movie, Mr. Welles.

WELLES: *(Performing a magic trick.)* It was a fiction, Miss Zadrov, make-believe.

ZADROV: Leni. A fiction based on fact.

WELLES: *(Performing another magic trick.)* A fiction with a little fact thrown in. Am I holding your interest?

ZADROV: Yes, you are. You're very good. Are you a professional magician, Mr. Welles?

WELLES: Orson. George Orson.

ZADROV: Where did you learn all your tricks, George Orson?

WELLES: My father knew Houdini. He taught me a thing or two. The rest I picked up in the Orient. I travelled there when I was a boy. I learned from gurus and mystics. They showed me how to charm snakes, and how to make things disappear.

ZADROV: And your mother? What did she think of your magic?

WELLES: Oh, well, women, you know, most women, they hate magic. It irritates them. They don't like to be fooled. My mother was like most women. She died a long time ago. Are you watching? Watch closely.

   (Welles performs another magic trick. And another one after that.)

ZADROV: God, you're crafty.

WELLES: Not really. How old are you anyway?

ZADROV: Ancient.

WELLES: Is Leni Zadrov, is that your real name?

ZADROV: No.

WELLES: What is?

ZADROV: I'll never say.

WELLES: Have you always acted?

ZADROV: Ever since I can remember.

WELLES: And are you acting now?

ZADROV: I am. And you?

WELLES: You don't think I'm Orson Welles?

ZADROV: I suppose you are, if you say you are, if you seem to be. I also sing and dance, you know. That's how I started.

WELLES: Would you sing for me now?

ZADROV: Oh, you wouldn't want to hear me sing.

WELLES: Yes. Yes, I would.

(Zadrov sings. And the world changes yet again. A party in progress. They are, for a little while, the happiest people in the world. Music.)

ZADROV: I've flown around the world in a plane

I've settled revolutions in Spain

The North Pole I have charted

Still I can't get started with you

Around the golf course I'm under par

And RKO has made me a star

I've got a house and a showplace

Still I can't get no place with you

You're so supreme

Lyrics I write of you

Scheme, just for the sight of you

Dream, both day and night of you

But, what good does it do

I've been consulted by Franklin D

And Greta Garbo has asked me to tea

You got me down-hearted

'Cause I can't get started with you.

Scenes for Men

AFTER DARWIN
Timberlake Wertenbacker
2 Men

Scene: Uncharted waters off the coast of South America, The Beagle, 1832.

Charles Darwin (thirty to forty), naturalist, and Robert FitzRoy, (thirty to forty), Captain of The Beagle, a devout Christian.

Scientific discovery clashes with religious dogma as these two passionate men square off aboard one of the most famous ships in human history.

> *Montevideo. FitzRoy's cabin. Darwin lugs some dusty bags. He is himself dusty, disheveled. The cabin is filled with dust. FitzRoy sits, very still, very dark.*

DARWIN: I rode with the Gauchos. They are so tall, handsome, proud, dissolute: long hair, black mustaches, clicking spurs and knives. So polite. *(He imitates a Spanish accent, rather badly.)* "Si, Signor Darwin . . ." but offend their dignity and — *(He imitates the slitting of a throat.)* I watched them catch their cattle with the lazo. Like this. *(He twirls an imaginary lasso.)* I tried it myself, but I tangled my own horse's legs and we both fell. How they laughed. Said they'd never seen a man capture his own self before. Ha. Ha. Ha. There was I, and the horse, both wrapped in the lazo like a naturalist's parcel —
(He falls on the ground to demonstrate. FitzRoy offers a wintry smile.)
We climbed the Sierra de las Animas. I found eighty different sorts of birds. I'll show you. All kinds of reptiles, even a ninety-eight pound water hog! The buck I shot had the worst smell I've ever encountered. I used my handkerchief on him, I think I can still smell it.

FITZROY: So can I.

DARWIN: We came to a salt lake of black mud, fetid. Ugh. I brought some mud back for you but I dropped the bottle. I'm sorry.

FITZROY: There seems to be some mud still stuck on your coat.

DARWIN: There were hundreds of flamingoes. The life, FitzRoy — on this seemingly grim and barren landscape. The flamingoes feed on worms, the worms on infusoria or confervae, all the life is totally adapted to this lake of brine, isn't it wonderful?

FITZROY: God's infinite providence.

DARWIN: Here's the best. *(He takes out some large and dusty fossilized bones with great care.)* I have many more coming. Wickham will be so cross with me. He can't find any more room on the ship!

(FitzRoy raises his eyebrows at this. Darwin places the bones on the floor as well as some teeth and a skull. It is all very heavy.)

Some of these crumble as you touch them, it's maddening.

FITZROY: Quite.

DARWIN: This animal was as large as a rhinoceros. The tooth could have belonged to an elephant. It's the tooth of a herbivore. And look at this: a neck like a giraffe's. *(He keeps placing and replacing bones, puzzling over the configuration.)* These animals are no longer found in South America. What happened?

FITZROY: The door of the Ark may not have been large enough to accommodate them.

DARWIN: Ha! Ha! Ha!

FITZROY: May I ask what amuses you so?

DARWIN: Surely, FitzRoy — Aren't you reading Lyell's second volume?

FITZROY: I run a ship!

DARWIN: Surely you agree with him that you can't explain all you find on high mountains by a catastrophic flood, but rather by a very slow — why, you said yourself —

FITZROY: I hadn't considered the consequences of such a statement. And Lyell fudges.

DARWIN: He proposes —

FITZROY: Waffle! Something must be one thing or another.

There was a flood: the Bible tells us so.

(A short silence. Darwin goes to another sack and brings out a dead mole-like creature.)

DARWIN: They call it the tuco-tuco, because of the sound it makes. *(He makes the sound: 'tuco tuco'.)* They're very friendly. *(He brings out a dead starling.)* A kind of starling. They stand on the backs of cows and horses. Listen. *(He imitates a bird sound with a bubbly hiss.)* It seems they deposit their eggs in other nests like our cuckoos. Now listen to this. *(He emits a high-pitched sound like a peewit.)* Just like a peewit, isn't it? Now. *(He imitates a pack of dogs barking. Brings out another bird.)* Nothing like it in England. Sounds like a pack of dogs in full chase.

(He does the sound again, intrigued. FitzRoy winces.)

Now, where have I put it —

FITZROY: Please! Stop it!

DARWIN: FitzRoy? Are you unwell.

FITZROY: I am perfectly fit!

DARWIN: I was so delighted with my discoveries I did not think to ask —

FITZROY: That is not unusual —

DARWIN: You have been working very hard.

FITZROY: Yes. Mr Geographer, while you were gallivanting about the countryside, I have measured, remeasured, and measured again every inch of this coast. Back and forth, back and forth — there will be no error in the charts of these waters.

DARWIN: Isn't that good?

FITZROY: Good, but not good enough. I have to do it again.

DARWIN: FitzRoy!

FITZROY: I don't expect you to understand the quest for perfection.

DARWIN: I am remiss for asking to take an interest in these fossils.

FITZROY: Please to remember I was the first to notice bones embedded in the silt off Punta Alta. Had it not been for me, you wouldn't even know of these animals. *(He puts his hands to his head.)*

DARWIN: FitzRoy?

FITZROY: Headaches.

(Pause.)

DARWIN: I found the country as hospitable as you described it, FitzRoy, but the Spaniards do not have anything like the sophistication of our English landowners. I also felt much disturbed by their policy of killing all the Indians and sending their children into slavery.

FITZROY: I once questioned a landowner on that very subject. He called in twenty of his slaves and asked them what they thought and to a man they said slavery was a good thing.

DARWIN: What else could they say in front of a man who could put them to death?

FITZROY: Are you questioning my judgment?

DARWIN: I am surprised you believed them.

FITZROY: But then your grandfather campaigned against slavery, I had forgotten.

DARWIN: What is wrong with that?

FITZROY: The trouble with meddlers like Wedgwood and other Whigs is that they do not know how other countries work. I do not say we should have slavery in England, but here —

DARWIN: If something is unjust and inhumane surely it is so everywhere.

FITZROY: It is a subject you do not understand.

DARWIN: I have travelled and I find slavery abhorrent and degrading.

FITZROY: You seem to take pleasure in contradicting me. *(He holds his head.)*

DARWIN: FitzRoy, you are not well . . .

FITZROY: It is the headaches that drove my uncle to suicide, he was never mad, whatever they said at your dinner tables — dinner tables . . . yes . . . the dinner we had at the Governor's house. I said everyone was reading Jane Austen. You demurred!

DARWIN: I only meant there may be some who do not read her.

FITZROY: You contradicted me in public.

DARWIN: But many Englishmen do not know how to read!

FITZROY: Everyone one knows or cares to know reads Jane Austen, Mr Darwin.

DARWIN: That is not everyone.

FITZROY: Again! You will drive me mad! I wanted the company of a gentleman. I find I am messing with a man who does not even know how to tidy himself before entering the cabin of his captain.

DARWIN: I forgot. I am sorry.

FITZROY: From now on, Mr. Darwin, I shall have to ask you to mess with the junior officers.

DARWIN: FitzRoy, you are out of sorts — you —

FITZROY: You will not speak to your captain in this manner! Get out of my cabin and take your disgusting specimens with you. *(He kicks a bone. It disintegrates.)*

APERTURA MODOTTI
Ellen Gavin
2 Men

Scene: The Spanish Civil War.

George Orwell (forty to fifty), author and freedom-fighter, and Vidali (thirty to forty), a passionate communist.

Here, Vittorio Vidali interviews George Orwell about his contribution to the war effort.

Vidali sits at a table. Orwell enters and walks before him.

VIDALI: Italiano?

ORWELL: No Inglés.

VIDALI: Orwell, George. What is your profession?

ORWELL: I am a writer.

VIDALI: Of what?

ORWELL: Fiction, history.

VIDALI: Useful for war. Military experience?

ORWELL: I served five years with the Imperial Police of Bunna.

VIDALI: *Filglie di putane.* At what rank?
    (Orwell is oblivious to the insult.)

ORWELL: The lowest. I don't believe in rank.
    (Vidali throws an AKA at him.)

VIDALI: Clean it, then load it.
    (Orwell fumbles at first. He breaks the rifle open. Grabs a bottle out of his back pocket and a self-made pull-through device from his pack. He pours the liquid on the rag.)

VIDALI: What's that, Orwell?

ORWELL: Olive oil.

VIDALI: *Non mi dici.* What are you, a soldier or a cook? Where's your gun oil?

ORWELL: Gun oil, are you serious, good man? Olive oil and bacon grease . . .
    only when we are lucky.

VIDALI: And what is that contraption? Where's your cleaning rod?

ORWELL: Hey I can run to the sergeant who's got the one battered ramrod we have in our division, and scratch the crap out of the rilling . . . or I can do it myself.

VIDALI: It works? Good enough. What training have you had?

ORWELL: Hand guns. Light artillery. I've been asking for machine gun experience since I got here . . .

VIDALI: When?

ORWELL: Ten months ago.

VIDALI: How many fascists have you killed?

ORWELL: Not a one. Can't say I'm proud of it. But that's the truth.

VIDALI: And you've been sitting in a trench for . . .

ORWELL: Five months, on and off on the Aragon front. If someone were to ask, "What have you done for democracy?" I would be obliged to answer, "I have drawn my rations."

VIDALI: Who's the capo in your division?

ORWELL: Aguirre. Basque. Sixteen years old. But he blew his ear off last week when he tried to fire a German Mauser, vintage, 1896. Only casualties have been, shall we say, "self-inflicted."

VIDALI: You mean to say you don't advance on the enemy?

ORWELL: Well, Christ, that's what I've been asking since I got here! We sit, seven hundred meters away from the enemy, they shell us, nothing lands, we fire back, knowing full well the bullets can't land anywhere within range. This isn't a war it's child's play.

VIDALI: What's your affiliation?

ORWELL: What party you mean? I'm fighting under the POUM. But I can't say that's what I am.

VIDALI: Well Mr. George Orwell, child's play is over. You just been promoted to Capo. O-six hundred, tomorrow morning, have your men in formation.

BAREFOOT BOY WITH SHOES ON

Edwin Sanchez

2 Men

Scene: Here and now.

Rosario (twenties) a young man fighting for custody of his unborn child, and Dr. Morton (forty to fifty) the therapist he's been assigned.

Rosario's temper has manifested itself in outbursts of violence against Vicki who is pregnant with his child. Here, the passionate young man defies the doctor's efforts to pigeonhole the source of his malaise.

DR. MORTON: Rosario, be a good boy. Don't.

(Rosario stares at the door where Vicky just exited.)

ROSARIO: Okay. I can be a good boy. I can be a good boy.

DR. MORTON: You still call her and hang up, don't you.

ROSARIO: I never . . . yes, sir.

DR. MORTON: I think it's safe to say she doesn't want to see you again.

ROSARIO: Yo don't know her like I do. I was her first.

DR. MORTON: Rosario.

ROSARIO: Fine. Just let her give me my baby.

DR. MORTON: You never married her. Legally it's her baby.

ROSARIO: Yeah, we'll see. You know, I don't have to come here.

DR. MORTON: Oh?

ROSARIO: She tried to press charges but she couldn't.

DR. MORTON: That's because your grandfather backed up your story that she fell down the stairs.

ROSARIO: Cause that's what happened.

DR. MORTON: You still take no responsibility for your actions, do you?

ROSARIO: You don't think we're gonna get back together again? Fine. You're the one who's gonna look like a fool.

DR. MORTON: Do you think I'm against you?

ROSARIO: Can I go now?

DR. MORTON: You didn't answer my question.

ROSARIO: No, of course not. I am loved and respected by all.

(Dr. Morton hands Rosario a paper cup.)

DR. MORTON: Could you please step into the men's room and give me a urine sample?

(Rosario stares at him.)

DR. MORTON: *(Continuing.)* It's a simple random drug test.

ROSARIO: I don't feel like peeing.

DR. MORTON: Luckily I'm sure we both have nothing better to do than wait.

(Rosario takes the cup and exits.)

DR. MORTON: *(Continuing.)* This is also a precaution for you. You're a window washer, what if you had some, let's say, recreational drug.

You might fall and kill yourself, worse, you might fall on someone and kill them. We have to think of those things. It's obvious that you don't. You seem to believe the world's problems begin and end with you. You are not the center of the universe.

(Rosario enters with the cup.)

ROSARIO: What did you say?

DR. MORTON: I said you have a lot to learn.

(Rosario shows Dr. Morton the cup.)

ROSARIO: Is this enough?

DR. MORTON: More than enough.

ROSARIO: You sure?

DR. MORTON: Very.

ROSARIO: In that case. *(He drinks a swig of his own urine.)* As long as it's more than enough.

(They stare at each other. Dr. Morton swallows, taps his clipboard. Rosario is about to leave.)

DR. MORTON: No, sit down.

ROSARIO: My hour's up.

DR. MORTON: I'm feeling generous today.

ROSARIO: I can't be late for [work.]

DR. MORTON: Sit. I'll call them.

(Rosario sits.)

DR. MORTON: *(Continuing.)* Perhaps you'd like another sip. *(Silence.)* Rosario, for future reference, I don't shock easily and there's nothing I hate more than grandstanding. Are we clear on that? Good. Now, your employers seem to be happy with your work habits. No complaints. You have no fear about working on the taller buildings?

ROSARIO: The higher the better.

(Rosario goes to the windowsill and sets himself up as if he were outside a window that he was washing. He continues to talk to Dr. Morton.)

ROSARIO: *(Continuing.)* It's a great job. I look in all these beautiful places and no one ever sees me. I'm like a fly on the wall. I'm invisible. I've seen people fight, make love and it's like I was never there.

DINNER AT DARIO'S

A. Giovanni Affinito
2 Men

Scene: Greenwich, Connecticut.

Mark (thirties), an operatic baritone, and Frank (thirties), a doctor and vegetarian.

Here, two estranged lovers finally reconnect.

MARK: *(Offers drink.)* Here. Have this first. Remember how horny vodka used to make me?

FRANK: Don't get overcome with nostalgia.

MARK: How I used to chase you around this very room? You didn't like *that* either.

FRANK: I know what you're trying to do. You're trying to seduce me. Do you know what the statistic is for gays reconciling after a break up?

MARK: You're going to tell me aren't you?

FRANK: It's practically nil.

MARK: Thank you, Geraldo Rivera. Now let's forget it.

FRANK: I'll never forget the time you left the cat alone in the apartment in New York. With the window open.

MARK: I was only gone for a half hour.

FRANK: If you were in the army you could have been shot for leaving your post.

MARK: For going to Bloomingdale's?

FRANK: It was the seventeenth floor.

MARK: Why can't you admit that there was never anything really wrong?

FRANK: That's a switch. You used to say it was my mother.

MARK: I still think Rambo had a profound effect on her.

FRANK: I only asked you here because I thought we both needed a sense of closure. Let's start acting like grown men.

MARK: Okay. Who's gonna play *your* part?

FRANK: Grown men, Mark.

MARK: I had this peculiar dream. What do you think of dreams?

FRANK: I don't go in for them.

MARK: Well, I had this peculiar dream. I'm in a city surrounded by water. Its gentle rhythm is felt everywhere. It's Venice, or Genoa. I'm standing before an easel holding a paintbrush and I'm about to paint something on which I know my destiny depends. An assistant is standing by and he looks like you. A happy you, mixing colors. A rainbow of colors. Then, with a talent I never possessed, I begin to paint in oils. I know they are oils because unlike watercolors, they have a feeling of permanence. As I continue I feel growing within me a sense of discovery, of joy, or something like joy. It's very physical. It's orgasmic, but spiritual too. Finally, what I've been painting begins to take shape and I could see what it is. It's the tree of life. Suddenly my assistant tears the paintbrush from my hand and I awaken.

FRANK: Is this about my life-stifling qualities? You won't tell Harold will you?

MARK: I think Harold would fuck up his own wet dream. And I don't think you have sex with him at all. Him, or anybody.

FRANK: Look. I wouldn't mind if you left now.

MARK: I can't.

FRANK: What's stopping you?

MARK: I never wanted to say good-bye at this good-bye dinner.

FRANK: We've talked this thing to a frazzle, and I'm sorry if I've hurt you, but you'd always known about my . . . problem.

MARK: I thought things would change for a while. Silly old me.

FRANK: Crying, praying, even therapy. Deep down somewhere I know there's nothing really wrong with me. I've just got to find the right voice in my head to tell me that it's . . . okay to feel good. One that I'll believe. Mark, you were wonderfully patient.

MARK: I used to dream about the kind of life we could have together.

FRANK: You're a regular dream pot tonight.

MARK: I liked the idea of having a lover ensconced in a nest and never having to forage for the food of love.

FRANK: Now you sound like a greeting card.

MARK: Who says I can't wax poetic about what might have been?

FRANK: I'm damned sorry, Mark. I'm so very, very sorry. I care about you . . . deeply, and your leaving was painful, but I would never stand in your way.

MARK: I know, but if you'd only . . .

FRANK: Look, when I was a boy, we had these chickens in a shed on the farm. I used to hug those chickens and cry myself sick, because there was no one there to return those hugs. It . . . kind of . . . numbed me. Understand?

MARK: Would it help if I wore a feather boa?

FRANK: You've been sarcastic, you've been a wit, but you've never been *trashy* before.

MARK: *(Crumples in the chair.)* Oh, so now I'm trashy too.

FRANK: *(Moving to him.)* My God, are you crying?

MARK: *(Begins to sob.)* Trashy indeed. What about you? You fall in love at the first hum of a Waring blender.

FRANK: I've never seen you cry.

MARK: I'll cry if I want to. Baritones can cry too, you know.

FRANK: Oh, that's not all you are. You're so much more than a baritone.

MARK: You're so insensitive.

FRANK: I am *not* insensitive.

MARK: You just don't really like men. Why don't you admit it?

FRANK: I don't like men? *Me?* I'm a doctor. I've admired more men in and out of their clothes than you've counted quarter notes. And y*ou!* I got soppy over you. Suffered like Romeo and bayed at the moon. But now I'm onto you. I'm onto all of you. The only thing you're capable of loving is a cat or a . . .

MARK: A chicken? *(Wails.)*

FRANK: . . . or a little dog. That's why I gave you the puppy. So you wouldn't die of loneliness, I gave you the puppy. I've *had* it, with your soft lips, your husky whispers, your muscular thighs, I no longer, I . . . I . . .

MARK: *(Suddenly stops sobbing.)* Well? Go on.

FRANK: I think . . . I got myself excited.

MARK: You mean . . . physically?

FRANK: Every way.

MARK: Well, *don't stop!* I mean let's wrestle or something.

FRANK: Wrestle?

MARK: Yeah, keep up the stimulation. Man to man.

FRANK: You're crazy.

(Mark tackles him and they fall on the floor with screams and gasps.)

MARK: *I hate you. I just HATE you!!!*

FRANK: *I'll never forgive you for this!*
    (They finally end up in a very prolonged kiss.)
FRANK: I love you.
MARK: You do?
FRANK: I love you.
MARK: Say it again.
FRANK: Oh come on. I love you. *(Pause.)* Well?
MARK: Well what?
FRANK: Now it's your turn to say it.
MARK: You love me.

IN MY HEART I KNOW I'M RIGHT
Galanty Miller
2 Men

Scene: The afterlife.

Lou (forties), recently deceased, and the Angel of Death, a Judge of Life.

When murdered Lou arrives on the other side, he finds that his life must suffer review by an unsympathetic angel.

ANGEL: Do you understand your situation?

LOU: Yeah but can I just say one thing before you do anything?

ANGEL: I'm not doing anything yet. You can say whatever you want.

LOU: Look, I don't know whether God thinks it's right or wrong, but in my heart I truly don't believe there's anything wrong with stripping.

ANGEL: Okay.

LOU: You don't sound convinced.

ANGEL: I don't know what you're talking about. I don't care either way about stripping. In fact, I guess I like it.

LOU: Then what else did I do wrong?

ANGEL: Nothing. This conversation is to decide whether or not your soul goes to heaven and you get rewarded. Something good may or may not happen to you, but either way, nothing bad will happen. You're not going to hell.

(Pause.)

LOU: Wow. You know, when I was alive I always felt this inner strength. Only it wasn't for me. It was sort of like a greater power was inside me, watching over me. And somehow I always felt safe.

ANGEL: You weren't.

LOU: No?

ANGEL: You were murdered. That's how you died. And that inner strength was confidence. Some people have confidence and some people don't. But it has nothing to do with us.

LOU: How come I don't remember?

ANGEL: Most people don't.

LOU: Why not?

ANGEL: Give me an example of something traumatic that happened in your life.

LOU: You mean like when I got my car broken into once, or something really big.

ANGEL: It doesn't matter — something big.

LOU: When my parents died.

ANGEL: So you remember when that happened.

LOU: Vividly.

ANGEL: Generally speaking, even the worst things that happen in your life you remember. That's because as bad as they might be, you can understand and conceptualize the incidents. In fact that feeling of safety you were talking about is bullshit because really, everyone always has a feeling that something bad is gonna happen. It's like when you're waiting for someone and they're late, you immediately imagine the worst possible scenarios — they were killed in a car crash on their way over, they were kidnapped by an escaped lunatic, whatever. When people look back at their lives, they always remember the worst things that have happened — the most traumatic incidents — above everything else. That's because the bad things make so much sense to them.

LOU: I don't know about that. I would think most people remember the happy moments, like when they got married or when their kids were born.

ANGEL: No, they only think they do. Yes, they remember they had a wedding day and they remember all the emotion that came with it. And yes, they remember their kids were born and that they were happy. Give me a happy moment from your life.

LOU: Am I gonna be judged on this?

ANGEL: Why do you ask?

LOU: Because the first happy moment I just thought of was shallow.

ANGEL: Tell me.

LOU: I had sex with one of my strippers. Not only was she beautiful, but it was the first time I ever had sex. I had been sort of a loser before that.

ANGEL: I know. And I also appreciate your honesty . . . I guess. Okay, so you took the stripper home and you made dinner and one thing led to another and you had a great time. Right? Okay, what did you have for dinner?

LOU: I don't know.

ANGEL: What was she wearing when she came over?

LOU: I can't remember.

ANGEL: In third grade, you were standing on the playground by yourself and these kids came over and started making fun of you. And you were scared.

LOU: Jimmy Tucker, Matt Burns and Ty Wilkins.

ANGEL: And then Matt Burns punched you in the head and you fell to the ground. And his friends were laughing. What was Matt wearing?

LOU: His yellow Little League jersey.

ANGEL: And then Jimmy Tucker pretended to kick you while you were on the ground, but he stopped right before he made contact. What was he wearing?

LOU: A blue T-shirt.

(Pause.)

ANGEL: We remember the bad things. Life is pain and while we may not like that fact, we accept it and understand it. And if you don't, you can't really live.

LOU: Okay, but isn't that the opposite of my situation. Getting murdered is bad so how come I don't remember.

ANGEL: Getting killed is bad but death itself is not. However, it's a concept you can't really understand. Nobody can. No matter how hard you try, when you're alive you can never accurately visualize the idea of existing without thought . . . Do you understand what I'm saying?

LOU: I've lost interest. So who killed me?

ANGEL: Cyrus.

LOU: You mean that dumb white trash? I thought he was in jail.

ANGEL: He was. He got out and within twenty-four hours he found out where you were and killed you.

LOU: Why?

ANGEL: I don't know. He was insane. He was homeless. He blamed you for his sister's death.

LOU: Great.

ANGEL: If it's any consolation, he's gonna have a very painful afterlife. And his life now isn't so great either.

LOU: No, it isn't any consolation. It isn't enough.

ANGEL: I don't disagree with you.

LOU: So is Cyrus my competition into heaven?

ANGEL: Cyrus isn't going to heaven.

LOU: Am I?

ANGEL: Do you think you should?

LOU: I look around at the people around me and if that's my competition then yeah, I think I deserve to get in.

ANGEL: You think you should get into heaven just because you're a better person than most of the losers around you? What about getting in on your own merits? (Pause.) But if you want to compare yourself, there are other people in the world who aspire to deeds greater than screwing strippers. Some people dedicate their lives to their families, or spend their lives helping the homeless.

LOU: So what.

ANGEL: That's gonna cost you points.

LOU: I was joking.

ANGEL: So was I.

LOU: But . . .

ANGEL: But.

LOU: If I can't compare myself to the bad people, then it's not fair to judge me based on anyone. Okay, so you spend a lot of time working in a soup kitchen or something — that's a nice thing. But you should do that for yourself. Or for other people. But in terms of what you should do as a human being for God, or for *you* specifically, you should do this —

ANGEL: First of all, nobody should ever live their life for God, and especially not for me. You should live life for yourself — but you should live it in certain ways.

LOU: Okay. Whatever.

ANGEL: Finish what you were saying.

LOU: This is how you should live — don't break any laws, respect other people's property, don't expect other people to pay your rent, and have as much fun as you can while strictly adhering to those rules.

(Pause.)

LOU: You don't agree.

ANGEL: That's a recipe for being a decent person. But is that all you wanna be?

LOU: What's wrong with being decent? Do you know how rare it is to find a good, decent person in the world? But we live in a society where even that's not enough. Somehow just being good is boring. It means nothing. And heaven, hell, whatever . . . I just want to be where the other regular, decent people are.

ANGEL: A lot of those regular people you're speaking about probably don't want to be with *you*.

LOU: Then I give up. What do you want from me? What was I supposed to do that I didn't? Just let me know.

ANGEL: What's wrong with expecting more?

LOU: More of what?

ANGEL: Your rules are fine. But not breaking laws and not hurting others — these aren't good things. Not killing anyone doesn't make you a good person. You're not *supposed* to kill anyone. So what is your life philosophy left with? Having fun. Do you honestly think, in your heart, there's nothing more to life than that?

LOU: No.

ANGEL: So all these people that do wonderful things are wasting their time.

LOU: No, not necessarily. But they should do what they do because they want to. That's what I mean. Do whatever you want, whatever it is that makes you happy.

ANGEL: I would rather watch naked people dancing than volunteer in a soup kitchen.

LOU: Watching naked people dance was my job. It was a fun job but it was still a job. But for most people, yeah, they'd rather see nudity than volunteer. But when they volunteer, they feel good about themselves. They do it because they think it's their calling or something. I don't know, either way it's no less selfish an act than going to a strip joint.

ANGEL: Give me a break.

LOU: It's true . . . Okay, maybe not, but it makes sense. And it's not fair to punish lesser pieces of the same puzzle.

ANGEL: What do you mean?

LOU: Everybody can't volunteer at a soup kitchen. It would get too crowded. The world works when some people work in a soup kitchen, some people attend AIDS rallies, some people spend their free time watching TV, and some people like to go to my establishments. I mean, the world has been around for a long time and it's still going strong. So obviously, we should embrace this situation.

ANGEL: Murder has always been around and the world is still functioning.

Does that mean the murderers are just pieces of a bigger puzzle and they shouldn't be punished?

LOU: So what happened to Swan?

ANGEL: She died.

LOU: I mean after that.

ANGEL: Nothing. She didn't go to heaven *or* hell. She just died.

LOU: She was a nice girl. How could she not go to heaven?

ANGEL: I didn't have anything to do with it. But if I did, I would have agreed with the decision.

LOU: Why?

ANGEL: Why not. She never did anything for anyone.

LOU: You know she had a terrible childhood — abused by all the men in her life.

ANGEL: You're eventually judged in terms of your own specific circumstances. But that doesn't mean you ever get a free ride.

LOU: What about the fact that she stripped?

ANGEL: What about it?

LOU: She was really good-looking and she got naked, giving joy and happiness to a lot of men . . . and lesbians.

ANGEL: Are you serious?

LOU: You said she never did anything for anyone. I'm saying, as shallow as it may be, she made a small difference in a lot of lives.

ANGEL: But she got paid for it.

LOU: So what. There are so few really good-looking people in the world. If you have the intellectual ability to cure cancer and you don't, let's say instead you become a lawyer or something, can't you be judged on that — I mean in a bad way? And if you cure cancer, but it's your job and you still get paid for it, it's still a good thing. Right?

ANGEL: Yes.

LOU: Well, then if you're good-looking, don't you have an obligation to use your looks to help people?

ANGEL: Going to a strip club is helping people?

LOU: It's making people happy.

ANGEL: Models use their looks. Should they all go to heaven?

LOU: They don't help people. In fact they annoy people. I say most models should go to hell.

ANGEL: Most of them will.

LOU: Except for the ones who pose naked.

ANGEL: So using your theory, what should happen to ugly people who strip for a living?

LOU: They should do everyone a favor and put their clothes back on. And don't punish me for that because I say it as a self-admitted ugly guy.

ANGEL: I wouldn't punish you for that. But why should you live your life based on the way you look? Physical appearance is coincidental and subjective.

LOU: If God made an appearance right now and said the same exact thing that you just did, I still wouldn't believe it. You *are* your looks. If a guy makes ten grand a year and gives a thousand dollars to charity, it has to mean a lot more than a millionaire who gives the same amount. In fact, if a millionaire only gives a thousand dollars to the less fortunate, that's probably a bad thing.

ANGEL: I see what you're saying.

LOU: No you don't. If I died when I was twenty, let's say I got in a car accident or something, what would have happened to me? Where would I have gone.

ANGEL: I don't know. You didn't die when you were twenty and you wouldn't have died when you were twenty. There's a greater plan which you can't understand.

LOU: But if I did. Up until that point in my life, I hated everything about life including myself. And I was this ugly little guy and I never hurt anyone. Yet were my actions, or lack of actions because I never really did much for others, the same as some handsome rich guy who also never did anything? Of course not. The handsome guy owed more because he was given more. Ugly people get shit on all their lives. As long as they're decent people, they should get an automatic entry into heaven. They don't owe the world anything. Fuck the world.

ANGEL: Life isn't fair. Why should the afterlife be any different?

(Pause.)

LOU: That was unconvincing.

ANGEL: Huh?

LOU: In my business, or in what used to be my business . . .

ANGEL: You can use the present tense. In fact I want you to.

LOU: In my business, you have to be part shrink and part mind reader. Everyone is out for themselves. And every other person is a crook, a thief or a liar. So after a while, you get a sense of what is sincere and what isn't. And that wasn't sincere.

ANGEL: What?

LOU: That "life isn't fair so why should the afterlife be" shit.

ANGEL: You think I really believe life is fair?

LOU: I *know* you don't believe it. You said it like it was something you're programmed to say — like something you're supposed to accept. But I don't think you do accept it. I have a feeling you don't accept a lot of the rules up here, or wherever we are.

ANGEL: You do what you have to do.

LOU: So who are you anyway? You don't seem like any supernatural angel or anything like that. Who are you and what are you doing here?

ANGEL: It's not something you have to worry about.

LOU: But I want to know. I think I'm entitled to know about the man whose decisions will effect my future being.

ANGEL: Life isn't fair. Why should the afterlife be any different?

MAN MEASURES MAN
David Robson
2 Men

Scene: A refugee camp in Macedonia, near the Kosovo border, the recent past.

Ben (thirties), an American doctor, and Agim (fifteen to seventeen), a young refugee with a terrible secret.

Agim has assumed the identity of a boy murdered by a cruel band of Serbs of Kosovo in order to gain sanctuary in the refugee camp. Here, the tortured boy finally reveals his awful secret to the American doctor who befriended him.

BEN: Tired?

AGIM: No. What?

BEN: I asked whether or not you're tired.

AGIM: Has bus gone?

BEN: It's gone.

AGIM: I am cold.

BEN: *(Handing him a blanket from a box.)* Take this.

AGIM: Don't we need to go back to tent?

BEN: No. Stay here. I'll come and bring you food when I'm not on my rounds.

AGIM: You do this before?

BEN: Hide someone in a hospital storage tent? Oh, all the time. *(Beat.)* I'm kidding. Now, try to lay low and nobody will find you. And when your mother comes —

AGIM: *If* she comes.

BEN: *When.* She's probably crossed the border by now. She could be here in a few hours. Don't give up hope.

AGIM: It is hard.

BEN: I know. You just have to hold on.

AGIM: Sometimes I think of killing myself.

BEN: Killing yourself? What are you — ?

AGIM: I try once already, but the gun slip.

BEN: Your wound.

AGIM: Yes. I do that to myself.

BEN: Where's this all coming from?

AGIM: It gets bad — *inside.*

BEN: There's nothing so bad that you should ever consider — things can change.

AGIM: Not here.

BEN: Anywhere. A person can always work toward a better life.

AGIM: You do not know. *(Beat.)* Is what happened to you?

BEN: What?

AGIM: With you and your wife.

BEN: I have to get back.

AGIM: But I want to know. Please.

BEN: It's no big mystery really. Jess wanted a baby — wanted it — I don't know — four or five years.

AGIM: And you wanted one too?

BEN: Jess would see a pregnant woman on the street and cry for hours afterward. She was jealous. And I couldn't blame her really. I was too, in some ways. It became apparent.

AGIM: What did?

BEN: You don't want to hear this.

AGIM: I do. Please.

BEN: It started taking a toll on our marriage — slowly, by degrees. So when Jess got pregnant three years ago I thought it saved us. That December, we had a little boy.

(Agim touches Ben.)

BEN: *(Beat.)* All babies are born with tiny holes in their hearts, but the holes usually close up right after birth. His never did. All those years, all that training, for what? When you need it most to find it's all so . . . so . . .

AGIM: The day is Tuesday. Family gets word from neighbors that police have told all Albanians to go from whole town. The family is surprised because these neighbors — Serbs — tell them in way to make it seem real — very real.

BEN: What is this?

AGIM: Maybe is all story. Maybe there is no mother. Maybe I do not have one.

BEN: You have one. I'm a doctor, I know these things.

AGIM: I must tell someone.

BEN: And it might as well be me.

AGIM: It can only be you, Ben. These Serb neighbors have lived next door for twelve years, but today they speak in ugly tones.

BEN: So does the Albanian family leave after the warning about the police?

AGIM: They stay. What can people do? They broke no laws, committed no crimes. TV is on and two small children — girls — their teenage brother, and mother are happy. What have they to worry about? And when threatened time comes and nothing happens, family — they have paid no attention to time — think it is all okay. Turn the channel.

BEN: This is your story.

AGIM: What happens next? What do you think?

BEN: The police arrive and drive the family away.

AGIM: You are moving too fast. Slow down. Enjoy buildup.

BEN: So the police arrive . . . and . . . ?

AGIM: One of the twins hears them first.

BEN: Twins?

AGIM: Family of four: Mother, boy, and two girls — twins.

BEN: And one of them is the first to hear?

AGIM: She is gone into kitchen for glass of water. It is hot today. The little girl sees one of policeman break kitchen window. He scares her so . . .

BEN: She runs and tells her family.

AGIM: You're ahead of me. The police have to come first. These police wear masks — not like police at all — the police carry no rifles or grenades — why would a policeman carry such thing? They barge in through back door while family sits on couch watching Bugs Bunny. They surprise one of twins, who drops her tall glass of water. Mother hears breaking glass and senses danger. She remembers threats of her neighbors and tells her teenage son to hide in basement. They will never hurt little girls, but young men must be hidden.

BEN: Am I missing something . . . ?

AGIM: How many stories have mob that does nothing more than scare people away?

BEN: So the family doesn't get driven out?

AGIM: Never.

BEN: They die.

AGIM: They die.

BEN: All of them.

AGIM: Someone has to live to tell story. So man of house — only sixteen — stumbles down basement stairs to hide just as police come into living room. There are ten of them. Without a word little girls are shot in head. Mother screams; she is punched in stomach. She goes down and crawls toward her murdered daughters. And now a man — your age, older — grabs her hair to get a grip before he takes out his cock. She screams when he gets on top of her, children's bodies nearby. Then, other men perform tricks silently . . . One after another finishes with her and goes toward street.

BEN: And you . . . all the while in the basement, listening to this.

AGIM: The last one — young, no beard — cries, doesn't want to. Boy is laughed at by first man, but others have gone and even first man forgets about young one's tears and he is ordered to check basement for more. He moves to top of stairs. And then slowly, like sleepwalker — A creak is heard in darkness, but where? Basement is small. It won't take long to find boy. I . . . I hear his breathing — like someone drowning far away — gurgle — catching breath. Then white. Eyes? I aim at white — I squeeze trigger three times quick. Bang! Bang! Bang!

BEN: What are you . . . talking about?

AGIM: Nothing. Nothing . . . It is calm now. Dark. I feel my way to him, find him then — touch his face. Still warm. Smooth, but beard not far off.

BEN: You . . . *you* killed him?

AGIM: Maybe I am just good storyteller.

BEN: What the fuck are you telling me?

AGIM: I have told you, Ben. I have told you everything.

BEN: What have you told me? What? You've told me nothing . . . This is what you did!

AGIM: It is what happens!

BEN: And what about the mother? What about her?!

AGIM: I would not let others kill her. Yuli wanted to. She is Agim's mother. I knew her . . . before . . .

BEN: Before . . . ? Didn't she recognize you . . . ?

AGIM: She could have.

BEN: And how . . . how do you know she's still alive?

AGIM: I don't.

BEN: But if she is — if she is, why would she come here?

AGIM: I wrote her letter, put it into one of book I had borrowed from her.

BEN: Books . . .?

AGIM: She had so many. Shelves full of books, but I made sure she would find this one. It was by Kundera — her favorite.

BEN: What did the letter say?

AGIM: It started as to say sorry for all we had done to her, but I wrote that her son gone and went to Brazde camp. That he escaped.

BEN: Escaped? She thinks her son — the one you . . . you . . . She think he's . . . alive?

AGIM: If your whole family was murdered, would you not believe — want badly to believe — and try and find him? If it was your child, would not you want it to be true?

BEN: But you didn't rape her? Did you? Tell me you didn't —

AGIM: Yuli did not pay attention. He was drunk. He thought I had, but I told you. I cried. I could not do it. I could not. *(Beat.)* I need to see her again. Explain —

BEN: What's there to explain, Agim . . . ? *(Beat.)* That's not even your real name, is it?

AGIM: I could not tell her then. Sorry that she had suffered and that twins suffered and that Agim suffered. I have to look in her eyes. I have to tell her this.

BEN: There's nothing you can say to her —

AGIM: Not for her. For me. *(Brief pause.)* Demush.

BEN: Demush?

AGIM: My real name.

BEN: And now they want to send you away to a family of total strangers in New Jersey.

AGIM: I cannot go there. Lumina is my only chance —

BEN: At what? Penance — ? Forgiveness — ?

AGIM: No.

BEN: What then?

AGIM: You do not understand. I thought you would understand.

BEN: Help me! Help me understand this . . . this fucking nightmare . . .

AGIM: I . . . I . . . cannot explain it any better, but I must see her. I must.

BEN: And where's Yuli — your friend? Huh?

AGIM: He was not my friend. Yuli died the day after we raided houses. A

NATO bomb hit our truck. It is how I got hurt. Please, I need you to
help me —

BEN: I've done enough. The moment you lied . . .

AGIM: What else could I do?

BEN: But you used me — a person I thought I had gotten to know.

AGIM: But you *do* know me — known me all along — here, in this place.
Between the two of us. We are friends.

BEN: How can you say that?

AGIM: A person is never one thing, Ben. I am Demush *and* Agim. The
moment he died I feel him pass into me. Demush and Agim. Agim and
Demush. Now, we are same thing.

SUNFLOWER TOWN

Kara Hartzler

2 Men

Scene: A small Midwestern town.

Luke (eight — but played by an adult), a boy who has stolen something, and Wayne (forty to fifty), the proprietor of a doughnut shop.

When Luke confesses his crime to Wayne, the older man urges the boy to start taking responsibility for his actions.

WAYNE: Hey there!

LUKE: Are there any left?

WAYNE: Any what?

LUKE: Any doughnuts! Any doughnuts left for me?

WAYNE: Doughnuts! We don't make doughnuts here!

LUKE: Yes, you do.

WAYNE: No, we don't.

LUKE: Yes, you do.

WAYNE: No, we don't.

LUKE: *(Pointing to the case.)* Then what are those things?

WAYNE: Those things? Those are vegetables we paint to look like doughnuts to fool little boys like you. See, this one's a zucchini, this one's a potato, this one's —

LUKE: But vegetables don't have holes in the middle!

WAYNE: They don't?

LUKE: No.

WAYNE: You're right. That's why we have to carve a hole in the middle of them.

LUKE: Wayne!

WAYNE: It's true.

LUKE: No, it's not!

WAYNE: I guess you're right. I suppose someone as smart as you deserves a doughnut, huh? Do you want a Long John or a bearclaw?

LUKE: Long John! I had a bearclaw yesterday.

WAYNE: All right, one Long John for the smart boy.

(Wayne retrieves a doughnut from the case and gives it to Luke.)

How was school?

LUKE: OK.

WAYNE: What'd you do?

LUKE: We learned how to make a cursive 'S.'

WAYNE: Uppercase or lower?

LUKE: Both. The uppercase one is hard. It looks like one of those clef things on a sheet of music.

WAYNE: The treble clef?

LUKE: Yeah, except it's backwards. Oh, and I pulled dead hermit crabs out of their shells!

WAYNE: You did what?

LUKE: The school had ordered hermit crabs for each of us, but something happened when they were sending them and they all came dead and the teachers didn't know what to do with them because they smelled so bad but we needed to save the shells for another batch of hermit crabs. So I told them I'd get the shells and I took a scissors and pulled every dead hermit crab's body out of its shell!

WAYNE: You did this during class?

LUKE: No, during recess.

WAYNE: So you skipped recess to dig dead hermit crabs out of their shells?

LUKE: Yeah!

WAYNE: What else did you do?

LUKE: I swang on the swing, and I swang so high that the legs of the swing were coming off the ground and making a thumping noise every time I swang and I was afraid the whole swing would fall over!

WAYNE: Sounds like a full day.

LUKE: Yeah! Did you sell a lot of doughnuts?

WAYNE: Pretty busy this morning.

LUKE: How come you're never busy when I come?

WAYNE: People like to eat doughnuts in the morning, but by afternoon, they don't think they taste so good anymore. But it's the same food, it's just a different time of day. People are funny that way.

LUKE: Like how no one eats salad for breakfast?

WAYNE: Yep.

LUKE: I also got these! *(Luke pulls four plastic letters out of his bookbag.)* See? I can spell my name with them. L-U-K-E.

WAYNE: Luke, where'd you get those?

LUKE: And then I can mix them up and make another word. *(Rearranges.)* K-U-L-E. Cool. *(Rearranges.)* L-U-K-E. Luke. Cool Luke. I'm Cool Luke.

WAYNE: Pleased to meet you, Cool Luke. Where'd you get the letters?

LUKE: They gave us letters to spell our names at school.

WAYNE: They did?

LUKE: Yeah.

WAYNE: So if I went outside and looked at the carpet store sign there wouldn't be any letters missing from it?

LUKE: I don't know.

WAYNE: I better look. It'd be a shame to have to give my doughnuts to another little boy every day, one who doesn't lie.

LUKE: But they spell my name!

WAYNE: Stealing is still stealing even if it spells your name. The Bible tells us that.

(Luke doesn't answer, just plays with the letters.)

Why don't you help me close up, and then we'll take them back and tell Wilmer you're sorry?

LUKE: I don't want to help close up.

WAYNE: Luke, we made a deal. You could come in every day and have a doughnut if you help me close up. I need your help. I don't want to have to find another little boy to help me.

(Luke gets up grudgingly, retrieves a broom and begins to sweep.)

So how did you swing on the swing if you were pulling dead hermit crabs out of their shells during recess?

LUKE: There's two recesses: one in the morning and one after lunch. I swang during the one after lunch.

WAYNE: What else do you do during recess?

LUKE: Go across on the monkey bars and see if I can go every other one.

WAYNE: Oh.

LUKE: Yesterday I went every other three!

WAYNE: When I was a boy, we used to play softball and tag and things like that during recess. Do you do any of that?

LUKE: No.

WAYNE: Why not?

LUKE: Because no one likes to play with me.

WAYNE: They don't? Why not?

LUKE: I don't know. But whenever I try to play with them, they just ignore me.

WAYNE: Maybe they don't know you want to play with them. Maybe you need to speak up and ask to play.

LUKE: I did that once.

WAYNE: What happened?

LUKE: *(Rearranging letters.)* L-U-K-E. K-U-L-E. Luke cool. Luke is cool.

WAYNE: What happened when you asked to play?

LUKE: They said we don't want to play with fags.

WAYNE: Who said that?

LUKE: Brian.

WAYNE: Do you know what that means?

LUKE: Yeah.

WAYNE: What?

LUKE: It's like a guy who hugs another guy.

WAYNE: It's when a man lies with another man in an unholy state.

LUKE: Like at slumber parties?

WAYNE: No. When they commit sinful acts together. Acts that are intended for a man and a woman in a covenant relationship.

LUKE: Acts that you and your wife do?

WAYNE: Yes, acts that my wife and I do to express our love to one another.

LUKE: So I'm not one?

WAYNE: No, Luke, you are not one. *(Pause.)* Let's go fill the mop bucket.

LUKE: I don't want to fill the mop bucket.

WAYNE: Luke, you need to learn responsibility. You can't come in and decide you want to eat a doughnut but you don't want to clean up. Part of growing up is learning responsibility.

LUKE: My mom said I need to get home early.

WAYNE: Well, if we both work quickly, you can get out of here soon.

LUKE: K-U-L-E. L-U-K-E. Cool Luke. Luke is cool.

WAYNE: Why don't you start filling the bucket in the mop closet and I'll bring in the soap?

LUKE: I don't want to fill the mop bucket.

WAYNE: Why not?

LUKE: I don't want to be one.

WAYNE: Luke, it's not the same. Where's your letters? Let me see your letters.

(Wayne rearranges them on the counter.)

See, you can take the same letters and make them mean different things. Like U-K-E-L. What does that say?

LUKE: I don't know.

WAYNE: Ukel! It's kind of like uncle. And you move two letters and what does this say? U-L-E-K.

LUKE: Ulek?

WAYNE: It sounds like a lick. Like when your dog jumps up and gives you a lick on the face because he loves you? Cool Luke gets a lick from his uncle.

(Luke doesn't respond.)

Luke, it makes me sad that no one wants to play with you.

(Pause.)

They don't understand what they're missing. You're a very good friend. And it would be sad if you didn't learn responsibility by helping me clean up. Because then you wouldn't be able to come in and have a doughnut every day. And you wouldn't have any friends at all.

(Luke fingers the letters and rearranges them.)

You start filling the mop bucket and I'll get the soap, all right?

Scenes for Women

THE APOSTLE JOHN
Jeff Goode

2 Women

Scene: A public restroom.

Mary (twenty to thirty) and Nikki (twenty to thirty).

When desperate Nikki encounters the spiritually enigmatic Mary in a public restroom, she is forced to put her immediate needs on temporary hold while the annoying stranger quizzes her on matters of faith.

Mary is standing in the bathroom, waiting contentedly.
Enter Nikki, somewhat urgently. She goes immediately to the first stall, pushes on the door. It is locked.

NIKKI: Sorry!
  (She tries the door to the second stall. It is locked, too.)
NIKKI: Sorry!
  (Nikki stands off to one side to wait. She looks around, antsy. She notices Mary, smiling benevolently.)
MARY: Hi.
NIKKI: . . . Hi.
MARY: You got a minute?
NIKKI: What? Why?
MARY: Do you have a minute?
NIKKI: No! I mean, why? A minute for what? What do you need?
MARY: I just want to ask you something.
NIKKI: Oh. Sure, okay. Ask me what?
MARY: Have you accepted Jesus Christ as your personal savior?
NIKKI: Oh shit.
MARY: I guess that's a "no," huh?
NIKKI: *(Looking for a way out.)* Uh . . .
MARY: Can I ask you something else?
NIKKI: You know, I'm in kind of a hurry. I really gotta go. I mean, I gotta

"go," and then I gotta get out of here. I'm right in the middle of this thing.

MARY: Yeah, me, too. . . . It seems like we're always in the middle of something, though, doesn't it? Lunch date, or a meeting or a lunch meeting or a conference call. Middle of work. Middle of school. Middle of life. No time. Not a minute to spare . . . No time for Jesus.

NIKKI: Yeah. Bummer.

(Long pause as they both don't look at each other.)

MARY: Did you hear that?

NIKKI: What?

(They both listen.)

MARY: There it is again.

NIKKI: What? What??

MARY: That silence. That's the saddest sound in the world. That's the sound of me not telling you about Jesus. And you not having time to hear me if I did.

NIKKI: Look, I don't want to get into this right now.

MARY: Oh, me neither. That's the last thing I want to do. But you really leave me no choice.

NIKKI: I leave *you* no choice??

MARY: You have to go to the bathroom, don't you?

NIKKI: Yes. No. None of your business!

MARY: What if it kills you?

NIKKI: What??

MARY: Do you know how many people die on the toilet each year? More than you'd think. Trying too hard, I guess. It's our competitive nature. Can't leave well enough alone. Gotta fight. Gotta win. Gotta . . . *(She gives a long scatological grunt, then . . .)* Bam! Pop an aneurysm and you're gone like that.

NIKKI: That's disgusting.

MARY: You think that's bad? Try dying on a toilet and then being cast into a lake of fire right after. That's really gotta suck.

NIKKI: Okay, that's enough.

MARY: I don't know you. You don't know me. After this, we may never see each other again.

NIKKI: Please, God, let that be true.

MARY: How do you think I'd feel if you went in there and dropped dead and I just stood by and didn't even try to throw you a lifeline?

NIKKI: Hey, I don't need a lifeline.

MARY: You don't need one? Oh, I see, you've got it all figured out. When the Judgment Day comes, you're just going to walk right up to the Heavenly Father and say, "*Look* at my schedule! When did I have time for salvation? Thursday I was in meetings all day, and Friday I had that lunch, and you know how tired I am at the end of the day, so let's not do it in the evening, and sure there was that minute I had in the bathroom, but that's my alone time. I need to focus. I can't have somebody looking out for my eternal well-being."

NIKKI: Okay, look, lady, this is neither the time, nor the place.

MARY: You're right. No problem. Why don't I catch you later then?

NIKKI: Good idea.

MARY: How about the next time you're in church? When will that be? This Sunday? Next Sunday? The week after that?

NIKKI: I don't go to church, if that's what you're getting at.

MARY: And you probably don't want me bugging you at the airport either.

NIKKI: NO, I don't want you bugging me anywhere.

MARY: So, it's not really the time or the place that bothers you at all, is it?

NIKKI: Yes! Yes, it is! This is a public restroom, for Christ's sake!

MARY: If only that were true. You know, they say that God is everywhere. But I don't think he's here. I don't think he's in a public restroom. You never hear stories about a good bowel movement bringing a person closer to God. You never see someone sitting in a stall with their head bowed in prayer, thanking the Lord for the precious gift of a clean urinary tract. God's blessings are all around us, everywhere you look, except here. Here it's just you, and me, . . . and temptation.

NIKKI: Now hold on!

MARY: You say this isn't the place for religion, but I say this room needs it more than anywhere else on Earth.

NIKKI: *(Knocking on the stall door.)* Hurry up in there!

MARY: *(Going for the kill.)* You're like the Lord Jesus Christ, knocking at the door to someone's heart, but she won't let him in. But what else can he do? He can't peek over the top. That wouldn't be right. But no one's answering, and he *has* to get in there. He can't slide under, can he? But maybe that's what the Lord Jesus is doing right now. Maybe he's sent me to slide under the door to the toilet of your heart to save your soul with his holy touch.

NIKKI: *(Backing away.)* Don't you touch me.

MARY: What are you afraid of?

NIKKI: I'm afraid of you creeping me out is what! I'm afraid this is a public restroom and I gotta take a pee and I'd like some privacy, but you're getting in my personal space and it's freaking me out!

MARY: No, I think what's really freaking you out is that you don't have Christ Jesus in your personal space. And without him, you're just a lonely sinner cornered in a dirty women's room by a dangerous psychotic who believes in crazy fairy tales and won't leave you alone until she makes you believe what she believes.

NIKKI: Yes! Yes, that's it!

MARY: But with him, you're never alone and you're never in danger because it's not crazy, because the fairy tales are true, and all you have to do is let yourself believe them.

NIKKI: *(Pleading.)* Please, just leave me alone, I'm begging you!

MARY: Will you accept Jesus Christ as your personal lord and savior?

NIKKI: Yes, yes, I'll do whatever you want!

MARY: Will you let him into your heart and into your soul?

NIKKI: Yes, anything, please! I just want to go to the bathroom.

(Mary falls to her knees and "joins" Nikki in prayer.)

MARY: Lord Jesus, hear this sinner's prayers. Fill her with the Holy Spirit, and grant her relief from her worldly suffering and a life everlasting with you in Paradise. We ask it in your holy name. Amen.

(Nikki is sobbing as Mary finishes praying.)

NIKKI: Oh God . . . Oh God . . .

(Then Mary crawls under the door to the stall and opens it from the inside. The stall is empty.)

NIKKI: What the — ??

(Mary gives the dumfounded Nikki a hug and walks out, smiling contentedly.)

ASYLUM
Kara Hartzler
2 Women

Scene: The office of an Immigration officer.

Leah (twenty to thirty), an idealistic young government employee, and Rosa (twenty to thirty), a frightened Guatemalan woman applying for political asylum in the United States.

Here, Leah interviews Rosa, a young woman who has suffered horribly in her native country.

LEAH: Se llama . . .
    (Looks at list.)
    Rosa Garcia Martinez?
ROSA: Si.
LEAH: Bueno. Siéntese, por favor.
    (Leah motions to the chair. Her Spanish is halting and stilted.)
    Soy Leah y trabajo para una agencia legal Proyecto Justicia. Proyecto Justicia es un grupo que brings volunteer lawyers from many parts of the country to come down to here and represent people seek asylum. The judge gave to me your name because now you not have a lawyer. So this morning I want to have with you a small interview about your case to see if help I can give you or we accept you as a client. This is all right?
ROSA: *(Whispering.)* Yes, this is all right.
LEAH: Firstly, I want to say to you that still am I learning Spanish, so I wish you have patience with me.
ROSA: I am still learning Spanish, too.
LEAH: What is your language?
ROSA: Quiche.
LEAH: You are indigenous?
ROSA: Yes.
LEAH: Well, we will try to understand each other.
ROSA: Yes.

LEAH: Where are you from?

ROSA: *(Pause.)* Guatemala.

LEAH: Of what part of Guatemala?

ROSA: *(Looks around the room.)* A town.

LEAH: How is the town named?

ROSA: I don't remember.

LEAH: Would you like that I close the door?

ROSA: Yes, please.

> *(Leah rises and closes the door.)*

LEAH: So for what reason did you leave your town?

ROSA: A man broke into our house one night and robbed us.

LEAH: Did you know him?

ROSA: No.

LEAH: Was he of the government, or perhaps the police?

ROSA: No.

LEAH: Was he of the guerrillas?

ROSA: No.

LEAH: Did he do hurt to you or your family?

ROSA: He threatened us with a weapon.

LEAH: What kind of weapon?

> *(Rosa doesn't answer.)*

A revolver?

> *(Rosa shakes her head.)*

A pistol?

> *(Rosa shakes her head.)*

A spoon?

ROSA: *(Confused.)* No, it was not a spoon.

LEAH: What was it?

ROSA: A knife.

LEAH: That's what I meant, a knife, not a spoon. Excuse me.

> *(Silence.)*

So what to you did he say?

ROSA: He asked if we had any money, and my father said no. Then he searched all through our house and didn't find any. Then he held the knife to my throat and left.

LEAH: Why did he hold the knife to your throat?

ROSA: I don't know.

LEAH: He said something to you?

ROSA: No.

LEAH: He only held the knife to your throat.

ROSA: Yes.

LEAH: *(Pause.)* Did he violate you?

ROSA: No.

LEAH: Did he return?

ROSA: No.

LEAH: When did you leave Guatemala?

ROSA: Two weeks after.

LEAH: And your family leaves also?

ROSA: No.

LEAH: Why does not your family leave?

ROSA: They were not as scared.

LEAH: The man wore a uniform or any kind of special clothes?

ROSA: No.

LEAH: He said to you he would come back?

ROSA: No.

LEAH: You receive a threatening note from him?

ROSA: No.

LEAH: Why were you scared so much that you leave your family when he did not come back or say he would come back?

ROSA: I was scared.

LEAH: If you are that scared, why do you wait for two weeks? *(No answer.)* I believe that you are truthful, Rosa. I'm just understanding.

ROSA: I had to leave.

LEAH: Why?

ROSA: My family would not let me stay.

LEAH: Why?

ROSA: I became sick.

LEAH: What kind of sick?

ROSA: A disease.

LEAH: What kind of disease?

ROSA: Venereal.

LEAH: *(Pause.)* Did the robber violate you?

ROSA: Yes.

LEAH: So your family said for you to leave?

ROSA: Yes.

LEAH: Oh, Rosa. How difficult.

ROSA: It's not important.

LEAH: You are sure that the robber was not a member of the government or the guerrillas or any kind of group?

ROSA: I don't know.

LEAH: *(Sighs.)* OK.

ROSA: You are a beautiful girl.

LEAH: What?

ROSA: You look like my sister and she was beautiful.

LEAH: Oh.

ROSA: My sister used to make beads out of clay and paint them red and blue and purple and string them together on a long reed. Then we would play Market. She would lay them on a rock and sell them to me. But I was so little that when she told me the prices I would cry because they were too expensive. Then when I was walking away from her market stall, she would follow me and say, "I am giving you this necklace because you are a sweet girl. Don't tell any of my other customers or they will be jealous."

LEAH: She sounds nice.

ROSA: She was.

LEAH: Well, I need to talk about with my boss your case, and she is going to decide if we can help you. Is there anything you need?

ROSA: No. You will return soon?

LEAH: Yes, and I promise to you that I'll do everything which I can to help you.

CHARLES DICKENS: A SYMPATHETIC STUDY

Dan O'Brien

2 Women

Scene: Here and now.

Wink (forties) and Berenice (thirties), sisters sharing eggnog on a snowy night.

Wink and Berenice have gotten a bit tipsy on nog and here share sad news and clever insights as they catch up on their lives.

Berenice and Wink, sitting in Wink's dining room. Nighttime, Christmastime, snow outside. They're both soused on nog.

BERENICE: I'm obsessed with biographies

WINK: Are you? I didn't know that.

BERENICE: Yeah. When they were born. When they died.

All the stuff that happens you know in-between.

WINK: Whose biographies?

BERENICE: Mine.

WINK: No, whose biographies do you like to read, Berenice?

BERENICE: O. You know. Famous people.

WINK: Do you like famous people?

BERENICE: Sure.

What does that mean?

WINK: What?

No, I just meant: "Wow, Berenice likes famous people."

BERENICE: Yeah.

Wow.

WINK: Yeah.

BERENICE: You think I should be reading what, biographies of *un*famous people?

WINK: Why not?

BERENICE: Okay. Do you have, I don't know, an autobiography of your life lying around —?

WINK: Don't be —

BERENICE: Or maybe your husband? He's unfamous. Where is he, by the way?

WINK: He's dead, Berenice.

BERENICE: Is he? I knew that.

WINK: No he's not dead.

BERENICE: I thought you meant euphemistically.
How old is he now?

WINK: He's not dead, Berenice, but he's got colon cancer. *(Pause.)* Can I say that after dinner?

BERENICE: O sweetie . . .

WINK: So whose biography are you reading now?

BERENICE: We can talk about it . . .

WINK: Whose biography are you reading now?

BERENICE: We can talk about it if you want.

WINK: *I don't want to talk about it. It's Christmas-time and I want to have a good fucking time!*
(Pause.)

BERENICE: Dickens.

WINK: Dickens! You're reading a biography of Charles Dickens! What a coincidence!

BERENICE: What do you mean — ?

WINK: Which biography?

BERENICE: You know them?

WINK: Try me.

BERENICE: W.H. Bowen, 1956, *Charles Dickens: A Sympathetic Study. (She cracks herself up.)* — Isn't that great?

WINK: Sounds — exciting.

BERENICE: It cracks me up every time — "sympathetic study" —

WINK: It's beautiful —

BERENICE: That's what I need when I'm dead. I mean, right? "Sympathetic study." Hell, I could use a sympathetic study right now.

WINK: Well sympathy is very rare thing —

BERENICE: That's right, sister — *real* sympathy, and not, you know, *pity* —

WINK: Or fear.

BERENICE: *Or fear!*

WINK: When I tell people about Ray, it's like they disappear. They go somewhere else, they might as well be phoning the conversation in.

BERENICE: I'm not going to pretend to know what you're going through . . .

WINK: Thanks.

What's he like?

BERENICE: Who?

WINK: Dickens. According to your book.

BERENICE: I don't know. What you'd expect.

Young Dickens in the blacking factory: "Please sir, may I have some more?" Dickens on the stage — he was a good actor, did you know that?

WINK: Yes.

BERENICE: He divorced his wife later, she'd gotten fat, and then he tried to marry this young tramp — that's what I'm up to now —

WINK: Do you like Dickens?

BERENICE: Sure. What does that mean?

WINK: Nothing.

BERENICE: You don't like Dickens?

WINK: Well, he was a very popular writer.

BERENICE: *(Laughing.)* O Jesus thank you.

WINK: What?

BERENICE: This is just what I've missed about you, Wink.

WINK: What, what have you missed?

BERENICE: Just because the man was popular doesn't mean he wasn't a great writer!

WINK: Well, see, I disagree with you there: He wasn't a *great* writer. He was a great *storyteller.* His *stories* were great, I'll give you that. But he wasn't a great *writer.*

BERENICE: You should've been a lawyer.

WINK: Take *Christmas Carol.*

BERENICE: All right.

WINK: Charles mentions —

BERENICE: What are you, on a first name basis with him —?

WINK: *Mr. Dickens* mentions, on page one, not once, not twice, but *four times,* that "Marley was dead." FOUR TIMES.

BERENICE: He didn't want you to miss it.

WINK: *Four times!* "Marley was dead," "Dead as a door nail," "Scrooge knew he was dead."

BERENICE: That's only three.

WINK: *"There is no doubt that Marley was dead!"*

BERENICE: Look: I don't care if he was a great writer or not. — Do you have the whole story memorized? I'm not an English professor. I haven't actually *read* any books by Charles Dickens, if you must know. I saw *Christmas Carol* once, in high school. I hated it. Except for the third ghost. I dug the third ghost — Ghost of Christmas Future. That *finger.* *(She shivers.)* And I read most of *Great Expectations* in high school, but I just thought Tess was such a ridiculous slut.

WINK: That's *Tess of the D'Ubervilles.*

BERENICE: Excuse me?

WINK: You're thinking of *Tess of the D'Ubervilles.* Thomas Hardy wrote that.

BERENICE: Hnh.

WINK: Yeah.

BERENICE: Well that's not the point. The point is, I love reading *about* the writer, you know, what kind of sordid condition their lives were in when they *made* something. I don't even care what that something was. It's the fact that they were every bit as screwed up as you and me, but they somehow pulled off something extraordinary.

(Pause.)

WINK: I'll drink to that.

BERENICE: Cheers.

WINK: Hey, Berenice.

BERENICE: What?

WINK: Would you like to meet him?

BERENICE: Who?

WINK: Dickens. Charles.

BERENICE: Sure.

WINK: What would you say to him, if you met him?

BERENICE: "Why'd you make Tess such a slut?"

WINK: No really.

BERENICE: I don't know. I'd have a drink with him. Get him drunk, have sex.

WINK: For real.

BERENICE: How do I know? He might be an asshole.

WINK: He's not.

BERENICE: O is he not? Shut up, Wink.

WINK: I'm going to tell you something, and I don't want you to think I'm crazy.

BERENICE: All right.

WINK: Hallucinating, grief-stricken, lonely.

BERENICE: Are you? any of those things?

WINK: Chuck and I are friends.

(Pause.)

BERENICE: Really.

WINK: Yes. We talk a great deal. He's a very interesting man.

BERENICE: I thought you didn't like his writing.

WINK: We don't talk about his writing. We just *talk.*

BERENICE: About what sort of thing?

WINK: Life. Death. He helps me remember what's important.

BERENICE: Which is?

WINK: You'll have to ask him yourself.

BERENICE: Charles Dickens knows what's important? Is he Buddhist?

WINK: He's good to talk to. He's been there, done that.

BERENICE: And where is he now?

WINK: In the cabinet.

BERENICE: Which one — this one, here?

WINK: I had to move the china out.

BERENICE: Is he a very small man?

WINK: Well he's not tall.

BERENICE: And you talk to him, what, how often?

WINK: During the day when Ray was at work, or sometimes at night if I was having trouble sleeping. But now that I've got the whole house to myself . . .

BERENICE: Wink?

WINK: What?

BERENICE: Do you think you might be . . .?

WINK: No.

BERENICE: Lying? to me? just a little? You always were a bit of a liar.

WINK: Open the door. See for yourself.

(Wink knocks on the cabinet door.)

WINK: Chuck? Love? Are you up?

BERENICE: All right.

WINK: You don't have to do this.

BERENICE: I want to.

WINK: Don't do it if you don't think you can handle it.

BERENICE: What's it going to do, explode my brain?

WINK: He's Charles Dickens, Berenice — he won't hurt you —

BERENICE: I'll do it. But listen: It's only because you're my sister, all right? It's
only because I know you. Here: Hold my hand.

(Wink takes her hand.)

BERENICE: Okay. Open it up.

(Lights up.)

CHIC BAND
Jaene Leonard
5 Women

Scene: Here and now.

Beaz, Dar, Geri, PK and Abe (all twenties), members of Chic Band. Young women with very specific dreams.

Following a practice session, these rockers kick back and play a favorite game called "Dream Session."

BEAZ: Okay, I call a Dream Session.
DAR: Must we?
BEAZ: Rules. I called it.
GERI: Dream Session?
PK: You'll get the hang. Check it out —
BEAZ: Check it out: Vehicles.
DAR: Dude.
ABE: Dig it.
PK: Right on. Go.
BEAZ: VW. Beetle.
ABE: Dude.
PK: New?
BEAZ: Old.
PK: Good. Those new ones —
DAR: — too cutesy.
ABE: Right?
BEAZ: Mint. Cabriolet. 1965.
ABE: Right on.
PK: Color?
BEAZ: RED.
ABE: Interior?
BEAZ: RED.
DAR: Rag top?

ABE: Cabriolet is a rag top.

DAR: Sweet. Red top?

BEAZ: White.

DAR: Yes. I can see it.

BEAZ: Right? Stewart Warner gas heater.

DAR: A heater's an amenity?

BEAZ: May I?

ABE: Shhhhh.

DAR: Just askin.

PK: Go on, Beaz.

BEAZ: Right. 5-spoke EMPI wheels. VW accessory under-dash shelf. 1500cc engine.

DAR: Cool.

ABE: Right on.

PK: I can see that.

ABE: I can see you in it. Okay. My turn. Vette.

PK: Dude.

BEAZ: Color?

ABE: White.

GERI: Sweet.

ABE: I mean. White.

BEAZ: Right on.

DAR: White.

ABE: White paint. White leather. White alloys. White fucking letter fucking steering wheel cover.

GERI: Dude.

PK: White.

ABE: White door handles, white body side moldings, white console and door panels.

BEAZ: White.

GERI: White. I can see it.

DAR: White.

ABE: White leather piping and Corvette emblem on the black fucking floor mats.

BEAZ: Dude. Woe.

PK: I can see it. White.

DAR: Is there such a white vehicle?

ABE: Yes. 35th Anniversary. 1988. Only 2,050 built.

BEAZ: T-top?

ABE: Targa.

PK: Dude.

DAR: Targa?

ABE: Targa top. Glass moon. Removable.

DAR: Sweet. I can see it.

ABE: The only car that ever made my mouth water.

DAR: Lotta car.

ABE: For alotta woman.

PK: Right on.

(They slap five.)

BEAZ: I can see it. Get you some.

(Another five.)

PK: Dudes. Dudes. Dudes. We get SIGNED.

BEAZ: PK!

PK: Check it out. It's a Vehicle.

DAR: Dude.

PK: We get signed. We get the cash. We ride into the sunset.

GERI: Como?

DAR: The object of the Dream Session is visualization.

ABE: Of tangible things —

BEAZ: Things we'll have when we've made the Go.

GERI: K.

DAR: PK's dream is ALWAYS to get signed.

PK: My main visualization is the signing on that dotted line.

BEAZ: And somehow it always fits.

ABE: Right? Somehow it fits.

DAR: PK's Dream Trip.

BEAZ: To the studio. To record for the label. To which we are signed.

ABE: PK's Dream house.

DAR: House mix. On the label. To which we are signed.

BEAZ: PK's Dream Man.

ABE: Manager. Afforded us. By the label. To which we are signed.

GERI: Which is the dream that PK built.

DAR: Right on.

GERI: So that's her turn?

BEAZ: Well, no.

ABE: She comes up with others.

PK: I fold under pressure.

ABE: But they're always slightly whacked.

DAR: Dream Trip:

BEAZ: Paris.

ABE: Via China.

DAR: Dream House:

BEAZ: Beach house

ABE: In the Rocky Mountains.

DAR: Dream Man:

BEAZ: Cross between Jared Leto.

ABE: And Lenny Kravitz.

GERI: Woe. Quite the dreamster.

PK: Right on. I Dream Big. Okay, dudes. I do have a dream vehicle.

ABE: Lay it on us, sister.

PK: Harley Davidson. FLSTC Heritage Softail Classic.

ABE: The softail. Fully dressed?

PK: Right on!

BEAZ: Color?

PK: Two-Tone Sinister Blue and Diamond Ice.

GERI: I can definitely see that.

PK: Staggered Fishtail Dual Exhaust. Laced wheels.

DAR: Man on the front?

PK: Dude. Man on the back.

ABE: Right on. That I can see.

BEAZ: On the back. Where he belongs. I can see that. Dude.

DAR: Can you ride?

PK: Dude. Ummmm. Shitcheah!

DAR: Cool.

PK: Check it out: I would like mine, por favor, with the 007 jet pack conver-
sion. Just in case I need to escape from some crazed fan.

DAR: Right on. I can see that.

ABE: Right on, PK.

DAR: Dudes. Dudes. Cessna 170B.

BEAZ: Como? A plane?

DAR: Dude. 1955. Barn-door flaps with the ten-degree setting.

PK: Woe.

DAR: 145 HP Continental Engine. Overhead cockpit pilot lighting. Fabric-covered wings, vee-type struts.

ABE: Dude. No.

DAR: Red pin on white paint. Swing-out access door. Molded leather interior. Mahogany woodwork panels.

BEAZ: Woe.

GERI: Dude. Can't see that.

ABE: Dude. I cannot support this.

PK: Dude. Nix the Cessna.

DAR: What?

ABE: We must say no.

DAR: What the fuck you mean by "you must say no"?

PK: Dude. It's the plane thing.

ABE: Dude.

DAR: Did I say no to your fucking Vette?

BEAZ: Dude. Buddy Holly. Curse of the plane.

DAR: What?

ABE: Buddy Holly. Ritchie Valens.

BEAZ: Stevie Ray Vaughan.

PK: That was a chopper.

BEAZ: Same diff. Air vehicle.

PK: Lynard Skynard —

GERI: Too many.

PK: Too dangerous.

DAR: Oh, and a fucking Harley isn't?

BEAZ: Not as.

DAR: And a convertible? Gimme a fuckin break.

PK: Dude.

BEAZ: Chill.

DAR: OH. I should chill. Meanwhile why don't you tell me what I should dream of.

ABE: Ah, jeez.

BEAZ: Dude. No planes.

DAR: All those people were wasted when they crashed.

ABE: Not all.

DAR: Most all of them. Were junkies. Or drunks.

PK: Dude. John Denver was not wasted.

ABE: Dude.

PK: "Annie's Song." Not a junkie.

BEAZ: "Take Me Home Country Roads." Not a drunk.

ABE: Dude. "Leaving on a Jet Plane." Straight as an arrow.

BEAZ: Dude. That was not John Denver.

PK: Dude it was.

BEAZ: "Leaving on a Jet Plane"? That was the Mamas and the Papas or some shit.

ABE: Dude. He wrote the tune.

BEAZ: I think not.

GERI: Whatever. "Rocky Mountain High." Nature was his drug of choice.

PK: And "Sunshine." He did do "Sunshine."
    (Pause.)

DAR: You guys, man —

PK: Dude. "Sunshine." Your all-time fave.

ABE: What?

DAR: PK!

PK: She told me.

BEAZ: Sunshine's your all-time fave?

DAR: NOT SO YOU'D TELL EVERYONE!

GERI: *(Begins to sing.)* Sunshine on my shoulders makes me happy . . .
    (Abe, Beaz, PK join in.)

ABE/PK/BEAZ/GERI: Sunshine in my eyes can make me cry.

DAR: *(Pause.)* You guys suck. And you're flat.

GERI: It's definitely a sign.

DAR: At least I don't like Celene Dion, Beaz.

ABE: You do NOT like Celene Dion! *(She moves away from her.)*

BEAZ: Dude. I said she has range.

PK: Dude!

ABE: That must not leave this room.

PK: Please. No. It'll ruin us.

BEAZ: DUDES! I am not a fan! I said she has range. That is ALL.

PK: No more talk of her. Second choice for vehicle, Dar?

DAR: Nope.

GERI: Dude. Come on.

BEAZ: Dream Session rules require —

ABE: You must participate.

DAR: Fine. 1979 Chevy El Camino.

GERI: Dude?

DAR: Forest green metallic, alloy wheels, 350 V-8, Navajo Wolf Spirit air-brush. Low miles. Cherry. With a kickin upgraded Bose stereo, sub woofers.

ABE: You are a thrill freak.

DAR: Oh, excuse me if it's not cool enough, Ms. White Vette.

GERI: Dude. That's a nice ride. I can totally see you behind that wheel.

PK: I can see it. My girl Haulin Ass.

ABE: Low ridin'. I can see that.

BEAZ: I can see it.

PK: Right on.

BEAZ: Your turn, Geri.

GERI: Woe. Mine dulls.

BEAZ: Dude.

DAR: You must participate.

PK: Dude.

GERI: All I want . . .

ABE: Yes?

GERI: Is a Lincoln-fucking-limo-con-driver to drive me anywhere my heart desires.

ABE: Is that all?

DAR: I can see that.

PK: I see it.

ABE: I'm seein it.
    (High five.)

BEAZ: Woe, I see it, too.

GERI: And you all can ride.

THE CONTENTS OF YOUR SUITCASE
Daphne R. Hull
2 Women

Scene: Train station in or near Paris, France.

Wren, an attractive lesbian, may have a British accent — or not. Colette, feminine, attractive, probably American.

A chance encounter outside a train station in Paris, reportedly the most romantic city in the world, leads two women down an unexpected path.

> *Wren is seated, reading a book. She also has a backpack and an obviously read newspaper beside her. Colette emerges from the train station, carrying two mid-size suitcases.*

COLETTE: May I?

WREN: Be my guest. *(Colette sits next to Wren. Colette arranges her things.)*
   Are you coming or going?

COLETTE: I'm sorry?

WREN: Are you arriving in Paris or leaving Paris?

COLETTE: Oh. Arriving — I've just arrived. *(Resumes her position.)*

WREN: Business, or pleasure?

COLETTE: *(Stops what she is doing once again.)* Er — both. *(Resumes.)*

WREN: Ah. Both.
   That's the trouble with everyone these days. Mixing business with pleasure. Sort of takes the pleasure out of travel. Don't you think?

COLETTE: Er — I don't — I don't necessarily agree, no. *(Resumes.)*

WREN: Single, or taken?

COLETTE: Married.

WREN: To a woman?

COLETTE: No! To a MAN.

WREN: Oh! Hm. I'm sorry, then! *(Colette resumes her position in a huff.)*
   I think there is a time for business, and a time for pleasure. Pleasure is a
   very, very important commodity. It deserves to be savored, without the

distraction of business. A solid foundation of pleasure can be a critical factor in determining success in business.

Do you know any small children who take their homework to the park, or the soccer field? Do little kids write book reports while feeding the ducks?

Of course not — and we adults help them keep things separate. But, as they get a little older, they fall into all our bad habits — studying at lunch, then skipping lunch, reading in front of the television, and so on. Someone decided along the way that we could be so much more efficient if we combined the two — business and pleasure — as often as possible. We lose the ability, soon enough, to focus solely just on one or the other, even when we really need to. And then, poof! Our childlike imagination crumbles beyond all repair.

COLETTE: It is JUST a little trip. I'll manage — imagination intact, thank you.

WREN: Oh, so you still have it, then?

COLETTE: Yes, I believe I do. There is hope for me yet.

WREN: I see.

There are lots of places to find pleasure in Paris, you know.

COLETTE: What time is it?

WREN: It's — it's a little after two.

COLETTE: Thank you.

WREN: How many children do you have?

COLETTE: You ask an awful lot of questions.

WREN: Am I making you uncomfortable?

COLETTE: You have been, since right after I sat down.

WREN: Then why are you still here?

COLETTE: I'm waiting for my taxi!

WREN: There are other places to catch taxis.

COLETTE: I'm not CATCHING a taxi, I'm waiting for my PARTICULAR taxi. It will be here shortly, don't worry.

WREN: I wasn't worried.

COLETTE: FINE. Well, neither was I.

WREN: I'm sorry if I make you uncomfortable.

COLETTE: Then stop doing it.

WREN: My name is Wren. *(Extends hand.)*

COLETTE: Did you say Wren? Like the little bird? *(Wren nods, hand still extended.)* You don't look much like a wren to me. Maybe a —

WREN: Swan?

COLETTE: Ha ha! Er — NO, definitely NOT a swan.

WREN: Peacock? Flamingo?

COLETTE: No, I was thinking of something more . . .

WREN: Common?

COLETTE: NO, that's not what I meant, I —

WREN: Maybe the scavengers — grackle? Starling? OH — I have it — a pigeon!

COLETTE: Ha ha, NO, I was thinking something more PURPOSEFUL, like a seagull, or a rooster, something along those lines. Not a pigeon.

WREN: Well. Fair enough. Thank you, I think.

Maybe you were right in saying you retained your imagination, after all. I'm still waiting.

COLETTE: For?

WREN: Your name.

COLETTE: *(Hesitates, grasps her hand.)* Colette.

WREN: Ah. Very elegant.

You know, you are much prettier when you smile at me than you were when you looked at me with all that suspicion in your eyes.

COLETTE: Thank you. *(Releases her grasp; it's been too long.)*

WREN: Your taxi hasn't arrived yet.

COLETTE: Thank you for pointing that out. It isn't due until half past.

WREN: Oh! So we have some time!

COLETTE: Er — time for WHAT, exactly?

WREN: For a game!

COLETTE: You're doing it again.

WREN: What?

COLETTE: Making me uncomfortable.

WREN: Sorry. But — just bear with me, this won't hurt a bit!

Here, let me see one of your suitcases.

COLETTE: WHAT? Forget it! *(Stands, grabs suitcases.)*

I'm going to find another taxi.

WREN: No, wait — don't!

I'm sorry; I should have explained myself first. I was too abrupt.

Please stay — I'm harmless, really.

COLETTE: I really should go.

WREN: Please. We'll use MY backpack, instead.

COLETTE: Well —

WREN: Please.

COLETTE: Well — *(Sits.)* all right. But one more false move like that, and I am leaving for sure.

WREN: Fair enough.

COLETTE: What time is it?

WREN: Twenty-six past the hour.

COLETTE: Not much can go wrong in four minutes, I suppose. Go on. Explain the game.

WREN: All right. It's not much, really — we try to learn as much as we can about the other person by examining the contents of her suitcase — in this case, my suitcase, since you don't like the idea of my rummaging through yours, and, also in this case, a backpack, not a suitcase, since I don't have one of those.

All right?

COLETTE: All right. Get on with it.

WREN: First item. *(Opens pack, removes an apple.)*

COLETTE: It's an apple.

WREN: I KNOW it's an apple; what does the apple tell you about me?

COLETTE: That you like apples?

WREN: Ah. I knew it. I was afraid of that.

COLETTE: What?

WREN: *(Sighs heavily.)* Your imagination has gone to pot, after all. *(Returns apple to pack.)*

COLETTE: It HAS NOT. Give me that apple. *(Wren obliges.)*

Now. Let me see . . . hmmm . . .

WREN: You are fondling my apple.

COLETTE: I am NOT fondling your apple!

WREN: Not that I MIND you fondling my apple . . . merely making an observation, you know.

COLETTE: I wasn't fondling — er — it must be examined properly, so I can get a good read on you . . . now stop that, you're trying to do it again.

WREN: Do what again?

COLETTE: Make me uncomfortable.

WREN: Oh — I thought we were past that.

COLETTE: Shush, I'm trying to concentrate. Hmmmm . . .

I need something else. The apple just is not working for me.

WREN: Give up, do you?

COLETTE: NO, give me something else. I'll come back to the apple later.

WREN: Well, it feels a bit like cheating, but hold on — here.

COLETTE: Seven pieces of chalk. Both colored and white.
Teacher?

WREN: No.

COLETTE: Hopscotch champion?

WREN: No.

COLETTE: Artist?

WREN: On occasion. That was very good. Nice work.

COLETTE: And the apple is a model for a still life.

WREN: Er — no. I was going to eat it, actually.

COLETTE: All right, give me something else.

WREN: All right. *(Replaces chalk, retrieves crumpled and well-used map.)*

COLETTE: A street map of Paris.

WREN: Good observation.

COLETTE: Well used.

WREN: Right again.

COLETTE: You either don't live here or just moved here fairly recently.

WREN: Yes.

COLETTE: Yes, what? There were two choices.

WREN: You have to figure it out.

COLETTE: All right, all right. Let me think. You are . . . hmmm . . . here on an extended stay, but have not actually MOVED here.

WREN: Excellent!

COLETTE: Really? I think I'm getting the hang of this.

WREN: Now. It's my turn. Give me something of yours.

COLETTE: Oh — all right. Hold on. *(Retrieves something in a very small box.)*

WREN: Do I have to guess what's in the box?

COLETTE: No — you can open it.

WREN: *(Opens box.)* A shamrock. You're Irish?

COLETTE: No. Look closer.

WREN: Don't give me any hints. That would be cheating. Oh, I see. Four leaves.

COLETTE: Right.

WREN: You are . . . superstitious. You believe in luck. Good fortune.

COLETTE: Fate.

WREN: Er . . . fate. Right. Me, too.

COLETTE: Hm. *(Wren leans forward to kiss Colette; Colette leans toward her, pauses, pulls back, and instead turns to take the box and put it away.)* Well. Okay. Next item? *(Taxi horn honks loudly.)* There's my taxi.

WREN: Oh.

COLETTE: *(Stands.)* Thank you.

WREN: For?

COLETTE: For the game.

WREN: Oh. You're welcome. Thank you for playing.

COLETTE: Do you — er — play this game with every woman who sits next to you?

WREN: Ha ha! No, no I don't. It is a highly selective game. You're the first, in fact.

COLETTE: I see. *(Taxi honks impatiently.)* Well. *(Wren stands.)* As long as I'm here — in Paris — you should — er — call me. Here. *(Hands Wren a card.)* So we can — so we can finish the game. *(Colette picks up her suitcases, gives Wren a quick kiss on the cheek, and exits.)*

THE GOOD GIRL IS GONE

Dolores Whiskeyman

2 Women

Scene: Here and now.

Lulu (twenties), a woman struggling to make sense of her life, and Ellie (forty to fifty), the mother who deserted her.

Ellie walked out on her husband and children when Lulu was 15. Haunted by her mother's betrayal, Lulu here confronts Ellie and demands to be released from feelings of guilt.

LULU: Mama . . .
  (Ellie nods, looks around, looks behind her.)
ELLIE: WAYNE!!
  (She looks at Lulu over her sunglasses. Looks behind her.)
ELLIE: WAYNE!! Bring the camera!!
  (She steps into the room.)
ELLIE: We should take a picture.
LULU: I appreciate this, you coming to see me.
ELLIE: It's all right. We're family. I'm going to sit down. Somewhere.
  (Lulu brings a chair.)
LULU: I was all set to come over. You didn't have to go to this trouble.
ELLIE: It's better this way. Wayne doesn't like too many people at the house. He's funny that way. Look out the door there, see if he's coming.
  (Lulu looks out.)
LULU: I don't see anyone.
ELLIE: Just like him. I tell him to get the camera, he disappears. What are you drinking here? Creme de menthe?
  (She picks up the glass.)
LULU: I'm not drinking.
ELLIE: You don't mind if I set one up do you?
LULU: It's okay.
  (Ellie takes a bottle out of her bag, pours a drink.)

ELLIE: You want one?

LULU: No thanks.

ELLIE: I buy only the best.

LULU: You always did.

ELLIE: Have one.

LULU: No.

ELLIE: Still a puritan.

LULU: No puritan.

ELLIE: You always were the goody-two-shoes.

LULU: No I wasn't.

ELLIE: Sure you were. Always had a book cracked open. Never went out to play. I used to rag on you to get out of the house. You just sat there, with a book in your lap. Wasn't normal.

LULU: That was Ginny.

ELLIE: Was it?

(She takes a drink.)

ELLIE: Maybe it was. Who can remember, that was so long ago.

LULU: You nervous?

ELLIE: No. Why would I be nervous?

LULU: Just thought maybe you would be. I would be.

ELLIE: No reason for me to be nervous. Is there?

LULU: So. How's Wayne?

ELLIE: When he gets here, he can tell you. Mind if I smoke?

LULU: Yes.

(Ellie looks at her.)

ELLIE: I'll open a window.

LULU: I'll still mind.

(Ellie gets up and opens the door. She lights a cigarette.)

ELLIE: Just like Wayne. First sign of trouble, he's gone. You married?

LULU: No.

ELLIE: Well don't get married. Twice I've been married — and believe me — it is nothing to write home about. It's all hormones, you know — you think you need a man. You don't need a man. It's just nature's way of fooling you into having kids. Otherwise, why would you? Nine months of dragging somebody else around inside of you, some little parasite sucks the nutrients right out of your bones — helps himself to whatever you got — and puts you through screamin' agony before he's done with ya — that is a lot like a man, come to think of it.

LULU: Aren't you going to ask about Papa?

(Ellie takes a drink.)

LULU: don't you want to know?

ELLIE: WAYNE!!

(A silence.)

ELLIE: Just like him, he disappears on me, when I would really —

LULU: You could really what?

(Ellie fills her glass.)

ELLIE: And how's your sister?

LULU: Not interested in what you're doing. I can tell you that much.

ELLIE: You came a long way just to be rude, you know. So why don't we get down to business? Me and Wayne wanna get to Wal-Mart before it closes.

(Lulu goes to the suitcase and finds an envelope, hands it to Ellie.)

LULU: Here.

(Ellie shakes it.)

ELLIE: No coins.

LULU: It's a check.

ELLIE: Just a little humor. That's what makes life bearable, you know. A sense of humor.

LULU: So that's the secret.

ELLIE: You coulda mailed it, you know. You didn't have to go to this trouble.

LULU: I could have. but then we would've missed this chance to get together.

(Ellie unfolds a letter and takes out a check.)

ELLIE: Damn.

LULU: You know Papa. He always was a saver.

ELLIE: In my whole life, I never could begin to figure that man out.

LULU: What's to figure out? He loved you.

ELLIE: Well, I guess so. Now I'm almost sorry I didn't make the funeral.

(Lulu slams the door.)

LULU: I didn't have anything to say about Papa's will. But if I did — you wouldn't be in it.

ELLIE: Well. I imagine it was a shock.

LULU: The least you could do is say you're sorry. You could at least say you're sorry.

ELLIE: But it wouldn't be true. *(Ellie gathers her things.)* I'm not sorry. I'm not happy about it, either. I'm just neutral, I guess. I don't know. To tell you the truth, I don't know what I am. I didn't really think about it. It just don't pay to think about things too much — you get along a lot better in this world if you don't think about things too much. Well. It sure was nice to get to see you again, but I guess it's time to go —

(She moves toward the door. Lulu doesn't budge.)

ELLIE: Are you gonna keep on standin' there?

LULU: Would you rather I didn't?

ELLIE: I'd like to get by.

(Lulu crosses her arms, doesn't move.)

ELLIE: Is this the part where I should get nervous?

LULU: What do you think?

(Ellie considers this situation, takes a drink.)

ELLIE: A little Jack Damage calms the nerves. You should try it some time.

LULU: What makes you think I haven't?

ELLIE: You are developing a strange habit of respondin' to everything I say with a question.

LULU: Does that bother you?

ELLIE: I knew this was comin'. Wayne warned me about this. You got some kinda agenda, don't you? This is where you start layin' into me about what a train wreck your life is because of me. Damn that Wayne — ten to one he went to the bar. Four o'clock in the afternoon, and that sonofabitch is at a bar . . .

LULU: I only have one question.

ELLIE: Let me guess. Let me guess. Why? Why, Mama? Is that it? Is that your question?

LULU: *(A little embarrassed.)* Yeah.

ELLIE: Well, why not? That's my answer is "why not?"

LULU: That's no kind of answer.

ELLIE: That's the answer you get.

LULU: That's not the answer I want.

ELLIE: Well, you can't always get what you want. If nothin' else, you should have learned that by now.

LULU: I was fifteen.

ELLIE: So? Ginny was twelve. And I was thirty-six and Wayne was twenty-seven and your father was — well, what was he, anyhow? I don't remember, but the point is — it don't make any difference how old you are when things happen to you — things just happen to you. I was three years old when my mother got hit by that car at the railroad crossing. And I got over it just fine. Why couldn't you get over this?

LULU: BECAUSE IT WAS MY FAULT!

(A beat.)

LULU: And I'm tired of it being my fault.

(Lulu locks the door.)

LULU: I want it to be your fault.

HAZELWOOD JR. HIGH

Rob Urbinati

2 Women

Scene: Here and now.

Shanda (twelve), the new girl at school, and Amanda (fourteen), a cute, romantic tomboy.

Amanda feels trapped in her relationship with Melinda, who dominates her life in every possible way. Here, Amanda reveals her unhappiness to Shanda, the new girl upon whom she has a crush.

SHANDA: Let's sit out here on the steps. I can watch out for my mom. She doesn't like me having friends over when she's working. 'Specially you because of the fight.

AMANDA: What you tell her?

SHANDA: She's just really strict.

AMANDA: What about your dad?

SHANDA: He's great. He lets me do whatever I want. But he lives in Louisville with my stepmom. I wish I could stay with him and have as much fun as possible.

AMANDA: My dad's real strict since my mom moved out. But he lets me have girls over anytime I want.

SHANDA: My mom doesn't like me around boys at all. I had the biggest crush on this guard at Skate World near where I lived and when she found out, she took away my skates. It's cause I'm — I'm only twelve.

AMANDA: Twelve? I thought you were at least thirteen. You look at least thirteen.

SHANDA: Thanks!

AMANDA: You have any boyfriends at St. Paul's?

SHANDA: Lots of 'em. Everyone thought I was boy crazy! I had to sneak around to meet 'em so my mom wouldn't find out.

AMANDA: D'you go all the way with any of 'em?

SHANDA: *(Possibly lying.)* Yup. But I never had a real boyfriend. That I loved. I don't think.

AMANDA: Shanda, can I tell you something? Promise me you won't get mad? Do you know who Melinda is?

SHANDA: Yeah, I love her hair. It's so pretty.

AMANDA: Well, um, Melinda and me are going together.

SHANDA: *(Matter of factly.)* Really? Is she Italian?

AMANDA: I don't know. Why?

SHANDA: She looks like this Italian girl I know. How long you guys been going out?

AMANDA: 'Bout a year. We met at a basketball game and pretty soon we was hot and heavy. We was seein' each other for three or five months before she asked me to go steady.

SHANDA: Isn't she like, really popular?

AMANDA: Everyone's just scared of her.

SHANDA: Is she conceited?

AMANDA: No, she's just crazy. My dad's kept telling me Melinda's a bad person but I didn't listen. She smacks me around for looking at other girls. It's messin' me up.

SHANDA: Amanda, if you're going through bad times and you need a friend to talk to, you can always talk to me.

AMANDA: That's so nice. You're so nice. I saw you when you was coming out for the fire drill today and I thought you looked so nice.

SHANDA: Thanks. I was in English when the alarm went off. I almost fell out of my seat! Then I had Basic Algebra, then Phys Ed, then lunch, then 6th when I see you. Then American Civics.

AMANDA: That's so nice, telling me your schedule like that. I gotta ask you somethin'. This might sound dumb, but do girls — I mean — do you like girls? I think it's cool 'cause it's so different. Is that why you're nice to me? Tell me — I won't laugh 'cause I think it's cool.

SHANDA: I don't know, I guess. You smell nice.

AMANDA: It's my dad's cologne.

THE MEMORY OF WATER
Shelag Stephenson
2 Women

Scene: Here and now.

Mary (thirties), a woman struggling to cope with her mother's death, and Vi (forties), her mother's outspoken guest.

All have gathered at the family home for Vi's funeral, but only Mary is visited by her mother's insightful spirit. Here, Mary and Vi discover that mother-daughter conflicts can indeed survive the grave.

VI: You look ridiculous in that.

MARY: The tin with the chrysanthemums on it. The one you don't remember. Where is it?

VI: I told you. I've no idea.

MARY: What have you done with it?

VI: You need a bit of colour on your face. You were always pasty.

MARY: Don't change the subject. Where's the tin? *(Pause.)*

VI: Have you tried the shed?

MARY: No.

VI: It might be in the shed.

MARY: I'll look then.

VI: Although it might not. It's been years since I saw that tin. It had toffees in it originally. From Torquay. I'd have liked to have gone there. They have palm trees. I've never seen a palm tree in real life. I expect you've seen dozens. You're probably sick to death of palm trees. *(Mary pulls on jeans and sweater.)* I do wish you'd wear something more feminine occasionally.

MARY: Apparently I look ridiculous. I'm going to look for the tin. *(She begins to go by. Vi stops her.)*

VI: This patient. The one you've got all the books about. What's wrong with him?

MARY: He got hit on the head and lost his memory. *(Vi gives a soft laugh.)*

VI: So what's the prognosis? Doctor.

MARY: He'll recover. More or less intact, I think.

VI: Intact. I like that word. Intact. Everything in order. In the bag. Right as ninepence. That's nice. Was he in a fight?

MARY: No, he opened a cupboard and a jar fell on him.

VI: Must have been a big jar.

MARY: Pickled bell peppers.

VI: You wouldn't get pickled bell peppers up here. Probably a good thing. They sound dangerous.

MARY: Can I go now? *(Vi has taken a dress from the pile.)*

VI: Look. D'you remember this?

MARY: No.

VI: I loved this dress. It was the only dress your father ever bought me. *(She begins to dance. It's slightly seductive and sensuous.)* Saturday nights I used to wear this. The men loved me, you know. Oh yes. All the men loved me. And I loved the men. I never cared for the women. I never liked them. Once I got my first bra I couldn't be doing with them anymore.

MARY: Pity you had three daughters really, isn't it? *(Vi stops dancing.)*

VI: You put words in my mouth. Every one of you does it, but you in particular, you mangle everything into something else. My comedy mother. My stupid, bigoted, ignorant mother.

MARY: Well you shouldn't say such stupid things.

VI: You lie in bed with your lovers and you tell stories about me. None of them complimentary. Most of them complaining. None of them true.

MARY: Excuse me. I'm going to look for that tin. *(She turns to go.)*

VI: Don't walk away from me! You've done that all your life. *(Mary turns round, like a guilty child. Vi picks up a book from the bedside table and opens it at random. Reading.)* "A biological memory system differs from a simple information storage device, by virtue of its inherent ability to use information in the service of its own survival . . . A library, for example, couldn't care less about its own survival. The problem is not one of storage. The problem is the difference between a dead and a living system." *(She shuts it.)* So there's a difference between a cat and a bookcase. I could have told you that. *(She looks at the price on the back of the book.)* Twenty-five ninety-nine. My God. *(Puts it down.)* I don't know how this happened. I look at you and I think, you've come out all wrong, all of you. There's something not quite right about how you've turned out. Not what I expected.

MARY: What a pity. After all your sterling efforts.

VI: You seem like nice, personable people. I expect you are, but I don't know what you've got to do with me. You're closed off. I can't seem to get the hang of any of you. You don't tell me anything. I tell you things. What I did, where I went. And you just look irritated. You've no patience with me. No tolerance. And I had years of patience with you. It's not fair. How dare you? That's what I feel. How dare you?

MARY: How dare I what?

VI: Sometimes when I'm talking and I know you're not really listening, I could tear your heads from your bodies. I could tear you apart with my teeth. All of you. You behave as if I'd no hand in the making of you. I took you on picnics, I got up in the night for you. And you remember the things you didn't have. Holidays not gone on. Bicycles never got. A particular type of shoe. How was I to know? When are we going to be done with this? I hear you talking and I think your memories aren't the same as mine. I remember the time of your childhood, and it seems to me that you don't remember it because you weren't there —

MARY: Why are you doing this to me? Why don't you do it to Teresa or Catherine?

VI: How d'you know I don't? *(She strokes the clothes left on the bed.)* All my lovely dresses.

MARY: I'm sorry. It's not as if you're going to be needing them. *(She begins to stuff them into black bags.)*

VI: You were in my bed with him.

MARY: He was cold. We didn't do anything.

VI: You wanted to.

MARY: Has nothing changed? You used to read my diaries, you knew about every boyfriend I ever had. You used to poke about my room. I always knew you were doing it, I used to watch you.

VI: I had good reason.

MARY: You did not. D'you understand? You did not. Ever. Nothing gave you the right to sift through my life like that.

VI: What is it you don't have? What's the word? Humility, is that it? I've watched you being offered the world on a plate. And all of it you've taken, without a backwards glance. Lovers, sex. Exotic sex probably.

Whatever that is. All tasted and discarded. You take it in your stride, these trips to Paris, these shoes from Milan, this bottle of wine and not that one, this man and not that one. This choosing and refusing —

MARY: You know nothing —

VI: I know different things. I know wanting and no choice. That counts too. It's not nothing. Excitement was a delivery of ornamental door-knockers. You drink champagne because you feel like it, you buy things with plastic cards. I've wanted that. I've tasted bile in my mouth with wanting it. And you carry it so lightly, you're not even grateful. I look at your easiness with the world and I don't know how I spawned you. But I started it. I taught you to speak properly, I saved you from your own stupid mistakes —

MARY: It wasn't stupidity, it was ignorance, and for that I blame you —

VI: I made sure you'd get somewhere, I made sure of it —

MARY: Your idea of getting somewhere was marrying a dentist in a sheepskin coat from the Rotary Club —

VI: You invent these versions of me and I don't recognize myself —

MARY: I'm not listening to you —

VI: I'm proud of you and you're ashamed of me —

MARY: I am not —

VI: I hear you say it all the time. I'm not like my mother. I'm not, I'm not. I'm like my father. Look in the mirror. Why can't you see it? Everyone else can. Look at the curve of your cheek, look at your hands, the way they move. You're doing it now. That's me. I got it from my mother. She got it from her mother. And on it goes, so far back that we don't know who began it or on what impulse, but we do it, we can't help it —

MARY: I've inherited some of your gestures. So what?

VI: Don't try and reinvent yourself with me. I know who you are.

MARY: You don't know anything.

VI: I look at you and I see myself.

MARY: Have you finished?

VI: Never. *(Go to black.)*

PRISON OF THE LOST SOULS
Kay Rhoads

2 Women

Scene: An old prison graveyard on northwest Iowa prairie.

Delphine Jay (twenty-five), an unbalanced convict, and Officer Gloria (forties), her guard.

Here, Delphine Jay searches for her mother's grave in an effort to benefit from some therapy prescribed by the prison doctor. Neither woman suspects the tragic conclusion that awaits.

At rise: Delphine and Officer Gloria West are in the prison graveyard. Delphine is walking slowly with a "witching" rod pointed toward the ground.

DELPHINE: *(Stops at a tombstone laying on its side.)* Look at this one, Gloria.
(Reads slowly and deliberately from the tombstone.)
Eeee . . . ve Cla . . . ra . . . Dun . . . woooood . . . y. Eve Clara Dunwoody. Born in pain. Died in . . . vain. December . . . can't cipher it out . . . nineteen and ought two. That's a long time back ain't it. You think it was a Christmas Day?
GLORIA: Such a tiny little tombstone.
(Reaches down and pulls the stone upright.)
There. You know, Eve Clara would have lived and died her whole life between then and now anyway even if she hadn't died right here in the prison.
DELPHINE: Could be some baby born here and died here on Christmas Day?
GLORIA: *(Gloria is walking away looking at other stones.)*
This place? Anything could be.
DELPHINE: I never even knew babies were even buried out here.
GLORIA: Lost souls of all sorts buried out here. Brrrrrr! Aren't you cold?
DELPHINE: Lost Souls. I like that. Nah, I ain't cold a bit. Colder the better,

you ask me. Plus, these folks underground, now they are cold, cold, cold. The lost souls are cold as cold can be.

GLORIA: They are dead, dead, dead. As dead as dead can be.

(The two laugh together.)

DELPHINE: So . . . o . . . phie With . . . er . . . spoon. Comed to Prison. Com . . . ed Comed to God.

GLORIA: *(Laughs.)* Close, Del, but that word is committed. Committed to Prison, let's see . . . ah . . . 1904. Committed to God 1922.

DELPHINE: *(Suddenly angry.)* Same thing!!

GLORIA: About time to call it a day out here.

DELPHINE: Look, Gloria, look at this witch rod, it's pulling me right into the ground so hard I can't hardly hold on to it none. Help me, I'm falling . . .

(Delphine struggles to hold herself upright with the rod pointed at the ground.)

GLORIA: Hmmmm.

DELPHINE: *(Sprawls on the ground.)* . . . and I can't get up.

(Laughs.) Okay, thy rod thy staff, release me.

(Tries to get up but gets the rod tangled in her coat.)

For serious I can't get up. I knew it, I knew it, it's like my preacher daddy said. Come feel this, Gloria. Thy rod cannot be risen.

(Gloria walks over to Delphine and takes the rod from her easily. She holds it up in the air and just looks at Delphine.)

DELPHINE: You don't have the true belief, that's it, that's what's wrong, if you don't believe truly then you can't count on it to work for you . . . because that's what my preacher daddy said and he should know.

(Gets up and grabs the rod back and continues to walk with it.)

Because . . . My doctor physician Dr. Rosemary said the same thing. Delphine Jay, she told me, if you find your mother maybe you'll find peace. And so I'm never giving up.

(Delphine bends to look at the stones.)

DELPHINE: My mama is out here and I got me a duty to find her. She cannot rest nor can I.

GLORIA: You know, Delphine, not everyone got a stone.

DELPHINE: That don't matter, she'll witch out anyway.

GLORIA: But maybe it won't be marked is what I'm saying.

DELPHINE: I'll still know. Is what I'm saying.

GLORIA: Well, I'll check some of these other stones. If I read the names out loud will you know which is your mama?

DELPHINE: I don't know her name for sure. Preacher Daddy said it might be . . . Mary Magdalene . . . or it might not be. He said she was here because that's where he had them put her when she was found out.

GLORIA: Madeline Mendenhal?

DELPHINE: My mama would not have a name Madeline Mendenhal. Do you think?

GLORIA: No, because this Madeline died in 1949. Before you were born.

DELPHINE: *(Laughs.)* My lordy yes. Maybe before she was borned . . . my mama Magdalene.

(Delphine gets up and begins to walk around holding the witching rod. The wind picks up and blows the hood from Delphine's head. She looks up.)

I believe, yes I do.

GLORIA: What did you say, Del?

DELPHINE: I was rent asunder from my mama. That's what I said.

GLORIA: What does Dr. say?

DELPHINE: Dr. Rosemary? She don't know.

GLORIA: She said to me that maybe you wouldn't find your mama out here.

DELPHINE: I know she said that to me too but . . . she wasn't sure was she or else I wouldn't be out here now nor neither would you.

GLORIA: She said a half hour.

DELPHINE: Ain't a half hour passed yet.

GLORIA: Almost.

DELPHINE: Almost ain't a half hour. A half hour is a half hour and the warden agreed with Dr. Rosemary if I partaked my meds which I did.

GLORIA: Well, they could have picked a warmer day.

DELPHINE: I like it cold. I like it cold as cold can be. *(The rod points to the sky.)* Look here, Gloria. My mama is in heaven.

GLORIA: Good. Let's go back.

DELPHINE: *(Laughs and points the rod down and leans on it.)*

Ah, I was just scammin you. Don't you know when one of us convicts is runnin a number on you yet? You been here long enough to tell that.

GLORIA: I been here too long. I lost my ability to ascertain.

(Both laugh.)

DELPHINE: Well, I ain't lost my ability to ascertain.

(Continues to walk around the graveyard with the rod.)

DELPHINE: *(Stops and begins to hum.)* Preacher Daddy weren't my real daddy. Did you know that?

GLORIA: I figured that.

DELPHINE: Did you ascertain that?

GLORIA: *(Laughs.)* I did ascertain that.

DELPHINE: My mama left me on the steps of his church. *(Delphine pushes her rod into the ground.)* The Church of the Lost Souls.

GLORIA: You're making that up because of what I said.

DELPHINE: I ain't. Ask Dr. Rosemary. The Most Reverend Preacher Daddy of the Church of the Lost Souls.

GLORIA: Mmmmmhmmmm. Where is it located?

DELPHINE: Located in the city of Des Moines, capital city of Ioway. Goin' up Sixth Avenue north of University, you know where the East Star Tap is? Above the East Star Tap. Closed up now. Boarded up and burned out I'm sorry to ascertain.

GLORIA: A church above a bar?

DELPHINE: Preacher Daddy used to say that's where the lost souls are, and he did go on and on and on about it, preachin and proclaimin . . . *(Raises her arms, the rod straight to the sky.)* . . . what better place in the whole wicked world to set up shop so to save some sinners.

GLORIA: He's got a point.

DELPHINE: That's where he found me. I guess I was about two minutes old, red and wrinkled and howlin like a banshee. A dark December day hours past lights out. Maybe Christmas Day. Like Eve Clara Dunwoodie. Cept I made it. I lived.

GLORIA: He raised you then.

DELPHINE: He raised me right up. With a rod like this here. Save the child, save the child.

(Silence. Delphine strokes the rod.)

He's black. Did you know that? He's black and I'm white. Didn't make no difference to him.

GLORIA: And your father?

DELPHINE: *(As though she didn't hear. Quietly.)* Didn't make no difference to me neither.

GLORIA: What?

DELPHINE: That he was a black man.

GLORIA: Five more minutes, Del. I'm freezing to death.

(Delphine breaks out into loud laughter.)

GLORIA: What?

DELPHINE: Freezing to death. Don't many people for real freeze to death. That's only something people say.

GLORIA: It does happen though.

DELPHINE: I suppose it do.

(The rod springs up and rigidly points straight out in front of Delphine toward the south.)

I declare.

(Begins to hum and walks toward the south.)

GLORIA: All the graves are right here. Last one dug and filled in 1958. You come on back now.

DELPHINE: *(Stops.)* Maybe my mama went to . . . one of them south sea places . . .

(Rod continues to rigidly point south.)

GLORIA: About when was it your mama died?

DELPHINE: I . . . My mama likely went to Florida.

(Turns her head back to Gloria. The rod remains rigidly pointing south.)

Because you're right she couldn't live in no frozen land like this here. She likely went to Florida where she figured she would send for me and then when she sent word to Preacher Daddy to send me on down why he wouldn't give me up because he always said I had a soul like would be in severe jeopardy outside the Church of the Lost Souls. His mistake I guess that was. He died hot.

GLORIA: *(Looks at her watch.)* It's time.

DELPHINE: Not frozen cold like Mama.

GLORIA: Delphine?

DELPHINE: *(The rod seems frozen in her hand and she doesn't move.)* Not frozen cold like Mama.

GLORIA: *(Approaches Delphine and gently touches her shoulder.)* Let's go back, Delphine. You're right it's a frozen land out here. She . . .

DELPHINE: *(Swings around quickly and the rod strikes Gloria in the face and lodges in her eye. Delphine startles and pushes on the rod. Gloria screams and tries to pull the rod out as she falls to the ground. Delphine looks at her.)* Nothin ain't out here but the dead. Held prisoner by the cold, cold, cold. Cold as cold can be.

DELPHINE: That Dr. Rosemary tricked me as I cannot witch my mama's grave in some frozen place.

(Gloria gasps and falls silent.)

DELPHINE: I didn't mean to do that.

(Reaches down and shakes Gloria.)

You shouldn't ought to have snuck up on me like that in the dark and in the cold you know that I don't abide any living thing to do that and my mama is not in some cold dark place such as this which is where my preacher daddy is and don't I know that since my soul was one he could not save so just get on up.

(Delphine pulls hard on the rod and it comes away from Gloria's body.)

This is not my fault, oh, they'll say it's my fault but then why would I do that? When I been lookin' for her all this time and here I was so close and now she is cooling down and freezing up so I should maybe give her my coat since it's bigger and warmer and since she's so cold.

(Bends down and touches Gloria's cheek and pulls her hand away.)

Oh, you are as cold as cold can be.

(Delphine leans down and removes the key ring from the officer's belt. She then takes off her black coat and covers Gloria. She stands there and begins to shiver.)

Mama, Mama, Mama Magdalene if that be thy name. You shouldn't left me on some church steps of the East Star Tap in the frozen cold of winter.

(She leans back down and smooths the coat making sure there are no wrinkles in the letter P. Unlocks the shackles and carries them off the stage.)

ROULETTE

Mrinalini Kamath

2 Women

Scene: Here and now.

Gina (twenty to thirty), a young woman sorting through the effects of her recently deceased uncle, and Loretta (fifty to sixty), her aunt.

Gina makes a startling discovery when going through Uncle Frankie's things. When she confronts Loretta, the two women are presented with a potentially explosive situation.

> *At rise: Loretta sits in a love seat with her feet on a stool, wearing a mu-mu and mule slippers. Standing on a small ladder by the closet is Gina. Gina reaches into the top shelf of the closet and pulls out handfuls of stuff, pausing briefly to look at them, before either tossing them by Loretta, or throwing them onto the floor on the other side. Loretta occasionally picks up something, looks at it with disinterest, then drops it back down again. Gina's accent starts out standard Northeastern and gradually, as she becomes agitated, migrates back to Brooklyn.*

LORETTA: Come on, Gina, you said you'd make me lunch.

GINA: *(Exasperated.)* Aunt Loretta, it's 11:00 in the morning.

LORETTA: Well, I ate breakfast early.

GINA: You were eating breakfast when I got here an hour ago!

LORETTA: Well, I'm hungry.

> *(Pause.)*

LORETTA: *(Pouting.)* You *said* you'd make me a salami and cheese sandwich.

GINA: Yes, I did. For lunch. It's still morning, and we still have all of Uncle Frankie's stuff to go through.

LORETTA: Ah, just put it in some boxes and give it to Good Will.

GINA: I can't believe you'd say that about your own brother. After all that time he spent looking after you —

LORETTA: Looking after me? Ha, I didn't need looking after. He was such a mooch.

GINA: Aunt Loretta!

LORETTA: Well, he had it pretty good here. No rent, home-cooked meals . . .

GINA: He ran all your errands, paid the bills . . .

LORETTA: With *my* money.

GINA: So what? You didn't have to worry about anything.

LORETTA: Oh no, I didn't worry about nothing, even though he could always
   get to my money —

GINA: Aunt Loretta!

LORETTA: *(Surprised.)* What?

GINA: He's dead.

LORETTA: So?

GINA: So you shouldn't . . . you shouldn't talk like that about him.

LORETTA: Ah, it's okay, I'm older, I can say these things.
   (Pause.)

LORETTA: I still say we give it all away.

GINA: All of it? You think Good Will really needs phone bills from *(Squints
   at the paper in her hand.)* 1977?

LORETTA: Who cares, let them sort through it.
   *(Gina just shakes her head as she continues to sort through things. She lets a
   sheaf of papers fall into the "throw away" pile.)*

GINA: What a pack rat.

LORETTA: Yeah, that was Frankie. It was like a disease, or something.

GINA: God, some of these things go back to the . . . wow, to the '50s.

LORETTA: What's so great about that? The '50s wasn't that long ago.
   *(Picks up a magazine and starts flipping through it. Gina just rolls her eyes
   and keeps sorting.)*

GINA: *(Unrolling a poster.)* What is *this*?
   (On further unrolling, she sees a 1940s scantily clad brunette.)

GINA: *(Amused.)* Wo-hoa, Uncle Frankie!

LORETTA: It's probably not even his.

GINA: What do you mean? It was in his closet.

LORETTA: It looks like a war pin-up, and Frankie was never in the war.

GINA: *(Re-rolling poster.)* Really? How come?

LORETTA: Perforated eardrum.
   (Brightening.)
   Just like John Wayne, he was 4-F for the same reason.

GINA: *(Rolling and rubber-banding the poster.)* So how did he get this?

LORETTA: Oh, Mike or Tony probably gave it to him. They brought him back a bunch of souvenirs.

GINA: Why? It probably just made him feel worse.

LORETTA: Nah, it made him feel like he was more a part of things. He was kinda lonely, your Uncle Frankie.

(Gina pulls down three photo albums and drops them at Loretta's feet.)

LORETTA: Well, what do you know . . . Frankie's old Boy Scout albums.

GINA: *(Continuing to sort.)* Uncle Frankie was a Boy Scout?

LORETTA: Uh-huh. He was pretty good, he made it all the way to Eagle Scout.

GINA: Wow.

LORETTA: Yeah, he really loved being a Boy Scout. I think it was the only place where he didn't have trouble making friends. Want to see a picture of him as a kid?

GINA: Ah . . . sure.

(Gina climbs down and stands next to Loretta, looking over her shoulder.)

GINA: Hey, someone's been cut out of this picture. *(Flips the page.)*

And in this one. *(Flips to another page.)*

And this one. *(Points these out to Loretta.)*

GINA: *(Pointing.)* See — "Frankie and Al putting up a tent." And in this one, "Frankie and Al, with their first big catch." "Frankie and Al in front of cabin 76."

LORETTA: Oh yeah. He and Al Cykowski used to be best friends. For years and years, they hung out together. Frankie was always sleeping over at his house. He brought him here a couple of times, but stopped because he and Al didn't "have enough privacy," since Frankie and Mike and Tony all shared a room. My mother said, "What do little boys need privacy for?" But Al was the only boy in his family and he had his own room, so Frankie would sleep over his house instead. They were always together, for like, four or five years.

(Gina goes back on the ladder and resumes the sorting.)

GINA: So how come none of his pictures are in here?

LORETTA: Ah, they had a fight and never talked to each other again. Frankie must've been 14 . . . maybe 15? He probably took 'em all out. *(Admiringly.)* He could hold a grudge, Frankie could.

GINA: Oh.

LORETTA: I sure could go for that salami and cheese sandwich about now . . .

GINA: It's only been five minutes, Aunt Loretta.

LORETTA: I'm hungry *now.*

GINA: *(Trying to change the subject.)* So he never even *talked* to Al again?

LORETTA: Nope. Al dropped out of the Scouts. Frankie stayed. Frankie had some friends, but not good ones. And he lost touch, so he didn't have many later. Yep, he just sat here at home.

GINA: That's so sad.

LORETTA: *(Annoyed.)* What do you mean, that's so sad? What am I, chopped liver? And speaking of liver, you *said* you'd make me a salami and cheese sandwich.

GINA: Oh, for God's sake —

LORETTA: Don't you take that tone with me, Gina Maria Perpetua Benedetti.

GINA: Never mind, I'm sorry, I take it back.

(Sighs, as she pulls down yet another box, small and white.)

Well, let's see what's in here.

(Pulls off the lid and drops it on the floor, then parts some tissue paper.)

Wow, a canteen.

(She comes down from the ladder and brings it over to Loretta.)

GINA: Look at that, it must be *at least* fifty years old.

LORETTA: *(Disinterested.)* Yeah, probably.

GINA: I bet it's a collector's item . . . or something.

(She carefully puts the canteen down on the table, then lifts out another layer of paper, and freezes.)

GINA: Oh my God.

LORETTA: What? What is it?

GINA: Oh my God.

(She tiptoes over to the table and gently puts the box down then tiptoes back.)

GINA: *(Almost whispering.)* There's . . . there's a *grenade* in there.

LORETTA: A what?

GINA: A grenade.

With the pin still in it. Oh my God, what do we do?

(Talking to herself as she begins to pace.)

First of all, don't panic. Whatever you do, don't panic.

LORETTA: What did you say?

GINA: *(Louder.)* I said, "Don't panic."

LORETTA: Who's panicking?

GINA: I'm about to . . . Aunt Loretta, we have an *explosive* here.

LORETTA: So, it still has the pin in it, right?

GINA: Yeah . . .

LORETTA: *(Nonchalant.)* So I'll just throw it over the bridge, next time I go out driving.

(Silence, as Gina stares at Loretta.)

GINA: *(In disbelief.)* Throw it over the Brooklyn bridge?

LORETTA: Yeah, why not?

GINA: I'll tell you why not . . . do you really think that no one's going to notice a grenade going off in the East River?

LORETTA: Oh please.

GINA: What do you mean, "oh please"? You think a fifty-year-old grenade with a rusty pin is going to hold itself together long enough to be carried out of this house let alone survive a car ride over the bridge? I don't think so.

LORETTA: Look, if it's been sitting in that closet for the past six years, a little more time won't matter. Just leave it on the windowsill. No one's asking *you* to throw it over the bridge.

GINA: Oh yeah, when was the last time you drove?

LORETTA: It's like riding a bike —

GINA: *(Interrupting.)* Fifteen years ago! I bet your license expired and you never even noticed.

LORETTA: So what? I'm not going *that* far. I'll just drive over the bridge, roll down the window and throw it into the river.

GINA: I cannot *believe* we're even having this conversation.

LORETTA: Oh, Gina, you always make a fuss over nothing.

GINA: Nothing! This is a live grenade.

LORETTA: Whatever. I think I'll take my sandwich now, please.

(Silence. Gina is really steamed, yet trying to stay calm.)

GINA: Aunt Loretta, we have to get out of here.

LORETTA: Not until —

GINA: We just *do*. We can't take any chances. I'm going to call the bomb squad.

LORETTA: — after you've made my salami and —

GINA: *(Exploding.)* How can you think of food —

LORETTA: *(Interrupting.)* I'm hungry.

GINA: HOW CAN YOU BE HUNGRY WHEN WE COULD DIE?!

(Silence.)

GINA: I'm calling 911.

(She's going over to the telephone; Loretta remains silent.)

GINA: Hello? Yes, I'd like to report a bomb. Well, a grenade, to be exact. Yes, the pin's still in it. Okay.

(Slight pause.)

Hello? Oh, this is the bomb squad. Yes, yes, a grenade. No, we're still in the house, but we're getting out. 145 Henry Street. Yes, we're leaving now.

(Hangs up the phone.)

Come on, Aunt Loretta.

(Loretta remains seated.)

GINA: *(Sighing.)* Aunt Loretta, the bomb squad's coming right *now.*

(Half-jokingly.) Geez, I wish I had known sooner that you shouldn't scream "fire" or "rape" in this city. Just tell 'em you've got a bomb, and they're falling over themselves to get to you.

(Loretta still remains silent.)

GINA: Aunt Loretta —

LORETTA: *(Calm.)* You go ahead, Gina. I'll follow you later.

GINA: What do you mean, you'll "follow me later"? We have to leave. Now.

(Pause.)

GINA: If this is about me promising you a salami and cheese sandwich, I'll get it for you after we get out of here and the bomb squad comes.

(Loretta is silent.)

GINA: Aunt Loretta? Do you hear me? I'll get you the sandwich later, but we really have to get out of here. That grenade could go off any minute.

(Loretta slowly shifts her position so that she's now lying on the love seat.)

LORETTA: Gina, I told you, if that grenade hasn't gone off for 6 years, it probably isn't going to go off now.

(She puffs up a pillow and puts it behind her back.)

GINA: Well, maybe you've just been lucky. You *and* Uncle Frankie.

(She goes to the closet and begins to close it and suddenly freezes, realizing something.)

GINA: How many years, did you say?

LORETTA: *(Settling against the pillow.)* What?

GINA: You said that grenade hadn't gone off in six years.

LORETTA: So?

GINA: So how did you know that?

LORETTA: I was just guessing —

GINA: Who guesses a number like six?!

LORETTA: I do.

(Silence.)

GINA: You knew . . . you've *known* that it's been here, this whole time.

LORETTA: I didn't say that.

GINA: Well, did you?

(Silence.)

GINA: I can't believe this. How many times have I been over here? How many times have I brought the kids over here? We could have all gone up in —

LORETTA: *(Interrupting.)* Have you heard of Russian roulette?

GINA: What?

LORETTA: Russian roulette. Do you know what it is?

GINA: Well, yeah . . . it's when you put a single bullet in a gun, spin, and then shoot. And if you die, you die, and if you live, you live.

LORETTA: Right.

GINA: What does that have to do with this?

LORETTA: This was our game of Russian roulette.

GINA: *Our* game?

LORETTA: Yeah. Me and Frankie.

GINA: *Uncle Frankie* knew about this?

LORETTA: Whose idea do you think it was?

(Pause.)

LORETTA: Well, it wasn't really *his* idea — he read somewhere that this writer who used to get depressed would go to the park and play Russian roulette. First he'd just go once a month, then twice, then every week —

GINA: But . . . why?

LORETTA: Because he was depressed and, well . . . bored. Every time he escaped death, the sun was a little brighter, the flowers in the park smelled sweeter —

GINA: No, I don't mean the writer, I mean you and Uncle Frankie.

LORETTA: I just told you.

(Silence.)

GINA: *(Sinking down on the floor in front of her.)* But what about —

LORETTA: He had nothing, Gina. I told you, no friends. He tried, but nothing ever happened. And since he never got married, no kids, no grandkids, nothing. And as for me, well . . . I was pretty much in the same boat. I never got married —

GINA: *(Interrupting.)* Why not?

LORETTA: *(Sighing.)* Because . . . have you ever gone looking for something, like, I don't know, a dress, and you know exactly how you want it to be, the pattern, the design, the fabric, everything, but you just can't find it?

GINA: Yeah, but . . .

LORETTA: And sometimes, *sometimes,* when you don't find what you want, you're willing to settle for something else, even though it wasn't what you pictured. You figure that if you like it enough that it might just . . . I don't know, *grow* on you.

(Pause.)

LORETTA: I had an ideal and he just . . . never came through that door. And there wasn't anyone that I *wanted* to grow on me. My parents were always asking me, "Why are you so choosy? At this rate, you'll never get a husband." And they were right.

GINA: I'm . . . I'm sorry, Aunt Loretta.

LORETTA: I'm not. I've never been one to settle for just anything, Gina.

(Silence, as Gina thinks about this.)

GINA: But . . .life's not that bad. What about the rest of the family?

LORETTA: Huh. Family. Family like you, off in the suburbs, hardly ever coming here to visit, unless you feel guilty? Dragging the kids along, even though they don't want to come?

GINA: That's not —

LORETTA: *(Interrupting.)* Oh please, Gina. I'm old, not stupid.

(Pause.)

LORETTA: *(Muttering.)* You don't even bring me a sandwich when I ask for it.

GINA: *(Not hearing this.)* They're never going to let you stay here, you know.

LORETTA: Who?

GINA: The bomb squad, the fire fighters, everyone.

(Suddenly we hear a variety of sirens, drawing closer and closer.)

GINA: They're coming now.

LORETTA: *(Getting off the love seat.)* Well, I guess I better get in the closet, then.

GINA: What are you talking about?

LORETTA: I mean, I'm staying, Gina.

(Silence.)

GINA: I'll tell them where you are.

LORETTA: Do it, and I'll never forgive you.

(Pause.)

LORETTA: Besides, it's not your decision to make.

(Silence. The sirens sound as if the trucks are pulling up, and then stopping. Loretta gets up and goes to the closet.)

GINA: You'll go to Hell, you know.

LORETTA: What?

GINA: This is suicide.

LORETTA: No it isn't. It's roulette. Only God's in charge of the wheel.

GINA: What do you mean?

LORETTA: I mean, if the thing goes off, then it was my time to go. If it doesn't, well, maybe He thinks I have unfinished business here. That I still have a purpose.

GINA: You do have a purpose.

(Silence.)

LORETTA: (Softly.) Thank you, Gina. Either way, I'll find out soon. You better get out of here. (She steps into the closet.)

LORETTA: Do me a favor?

GINA: What?

LORETTA: Close the door.

(Gina hesitates, then goes to the closet and gently closes the door and runs out. Blackout.)

SUNDAY SUGAR
Joanna Piucci
2 Women

Scene: Interior of an automobile.

Beth (twenties), a young woman on her way home, and Sheila (forties), a hitchhiker.

Here, two very different women bond while sharing a slice of roadway and some poignant moments.

Beth, the driver, lights a cigarette.

SHEILA: Do you really have to do that?

BETH: What, smoke? It's my car.

SHEILA: Your life, Honey. Your funeral, too, I might add.

BETH: Oh, chill, would you? Come on, I'm giving you a ride. Be grateful. How many people pick up hitchhikers nowadays?

SHEILA: A woman hitching alone? I'd have had a ride, don't kid yourself. But don't get me wrong, Sweetie, I am grateful . . . that it was you who picked up, and not some sleazy guy.

BETH: Good. Anyway, we all have our vices; I'm sure you have yours. *(She gives the passenger a once-over.)* Let's see, let me guess . . . drinker?

SHEILA: Never touch it.

BETH: Mary Jane?

SHEILA: Doesn't agree with me.

BETH: Sweet tooth?

SHEILA: I'm a diabetic.

BETH: Oh, I'm so sorry!

SHEILA: What for? I control what I eat. Big deal. *(Pause.)* I do have a secret vice, though.

BETH: What's that?

SHEILA: *(She stares at the driver for a few moments.)* Guess . . .

BETH: No thanks, I'll pass. Besides, you said it was secret.

SHEILA: Everything's secret, Sugar, until you reveal it.

BETH: *(She puts out her cigarette.)* My mother had that, too.

SHEILA: Um . . . are we talking about diabetes?

BETH: *(Pause.)* She died last year.

SHEILA: Oh, Honey, now *I'm* sorry, really.

BETH: It's okay. Well, no, it was rough, but I mean we're okay now. My Dad had us worried for awhile, but he's back to himself, even trying new things. I'm on my way to see him right now. He invited me for Sunday dinner. He asked my younger sister and her family, too. Says he's roasting a turkey. To the best of my knowledge, he's never cooked before, so I guess we're all kind of nervous.

SHEILA: How'd your Mom die?

BETH: You don't want to know.

SHEILA: Tell me.

BETH: Believe me, you don't want me to.

SHEILA: It had something to do with her diabetes, right?

BETH: Yes, but it was more than that. Oh, what the heck, I'll never see you again after today, right? *(They both laugh.)* Where should I start? *(Sigh.)* My Mom was a . . . well, a career housewife. You know, totally into her house and her kids, not much else going on. I was the oldest and the first to leave, and I didn't even go very far . . . just moved to my own place a couple of blocks away. But it threw her. She started focusing all her attention on my younger sister, Janie, and it got kind of . . . obsessive. She never even talked about anything else, but she'd talk and talk about any little detail of Janie's life. If Janie went out on a date, Mom would get all blue and mopey. But then when she came home, Mom would want to hear all the details. Eventually my sister married a guy in the Army and had no choice but to move to where he was stationed. They were gone two years.

SHEILA: Your Mom must have freaked out.

BETH: At first I thought she was all right, but Dad told me he didn't think she was making the adjustment. I kept waiting for her to find a hobby, do some volunteering, something like that. But it didn't happen. Instead, she cooked more food than she and Dad could eat, knitted afghans no one would ever use, and wrote letters to Janie . . . nothing else. I didn't visit often . . . I guess I figured if I did, she'd be even less motivated to leave the house. Then one morning I got a call from her:

"Beth, guess what I did . . . I just ate three jelly doughnuts." I dropped everything and ran up the street. I called the doctor from her house. Afterwards I asked her why she had done it . . . Mom had always been very responsible about her diet . . . and she said, "Oh, I don't know, Beth, I just felt so lonely today!"

SHEILA: She survived?

BETH: Yes, but after that she'd pull some similar stunt every once in a while. When Janie came back to town, I moved farther away. I just couldn't take it anymore.

SHEILA: No one can blame you, Honey, it sounds like she was leaning way too hard. It makes a great story though, you know? I mean, you always hear about people threatening suicide to get attention, but to do it with jelly doughnuts! (They both laugh.) I think that's what redeems some of our worst moments, don't you? That they make the best stories. So, what happened once your sister came back?

BETH: According to my sister, Mom was fine for a while. She had plenty to occupy her, taking Janie shopping, helping her to decorate the house . . . Then Janie got pregnant, and Mom really got into it, knitting layettes, buying toys. But the last month of her pregnancy, my sister was really uncomfortable. She got so she didn't much like being around people. She started to feel smothered by Mom's attention, and so she spent less time with her. She'd say, "Mom, it isn't about you, I just want to be alone right now." You have to realize . . . what's your name?

SHEILA: Sheila.

BETH: I'm Beth. As I was saying, you have to understand, Sheila, that my Mom had probably never wanted to be alone a single day in her life, so she just couldn't comprehend this. Janie went into labor a week early, in the morning, and her husband rushed her to the hospital, so no one was home when Mom tried to call . . . at least we all assumed she was trying to call Janie. Dad was at work, and by the time he came home and found her, Mom was in a coma, with the phone off the hook and a box of jelly doughnuts on the kitchen counter. She died a few days later, from "complications of diabetes."

SHEILA: Whew! How'd your sister take it?

BETH: Well, of course she felt enormously guilty, but all things considered, she coped pretty well. I guess having an infant to look after puts a limit on the time you can spend wallowing in self-blame.

SHEILA: You have any kids?

BETH: No. I'm not married. I lived with a guy for a few years, but it didn't work out in the end. And you?

SHEILA: No, Sweetie, no kids, just a history of long-term, neurotic and very intense relationships with highly inappropriate people. Right now I'm unattached. Foundering.

BETH: Are your parents still alive?

SHEILA: My father died when I was twenty, my mother when I was even younger.

BETH: How young?

SHEILA: Fourteen.

BETH: Tough age. What was she like?

SHEILA: She was completely nuts.

BETH: You mean quirky?

SHEILA: *(She laughs.)* Sugar, quirky doesn't even begin to cover it. She was seriously demented, from at least the time of my birth, though it probably started even earlier. After I was born she sank into a severe depression that lasted two years. Back then they didn't understand depression very well, so what little treatment she got was . . . rudimentary and ineffective. Her doctor was a country G.P. who prescribed long walks as a way of "changing her perspective." I don't remember this, of course, but I can't imagine she had much to offer me as a baby when she herself could barely function. Even after the depression lifted, she was never what you could call normal, at least not for long periods of time. Her behavior was erratic. For a while she'd be the perfect Fifties Mom . . . frilly apron, chocolate-chip cookies, singing as she dusted, the whole bit. And then one day I'd come home from school and she'd be at the kitchen table, still in her nightgown, breakfast dishes in the sink, a cold cup of coffee in front of her. I'd talk to her, yell at her, and she wouldn't respond. I'd shake her and she'd just hang her head. So I'd call my father, and he'd call the doctor, and Mother would spend a week or two in the hospital while I did the housework and cooked dinner for my father . . . all at the ripe old age of ten.

BETH: You must have been scared to death.

SHEILA: Of course I was. I think what was scariest to me was how unreachable my mother was during those phases. Where was she? That's what I'd ask myself. I could have stuck pins in her and she wouldn't have known.

She was like that off and on for years, then she started developing other symptoms. She'd have these odd little seizures . . . her mouth would drop open and she'd just stare at you for a few seconds, and then her head would swing slowly to the left, as if someone was tugging on her chin. In a minute or so she'd snap out of it, but she'd be all confused. They ran some tests and discovered a brain tumor. She died a few months after they found it.

BETH: Do you think that was the cause of her problems all along?

SHEILA: Oh, it may have been, but I never could get a doctor to say one way or the other. I don't suppose it really matters.

BETH: When did you find out you were diabetic?

SHEILA: When I was twelve. My mother really tried to pull it together to help me, but she just couldn't do it. Basically I had to handle it on my own.

BETH: Your dad?

SHEILA: My father was always busy. This is no exaggeration, Sweetie, I raised myself, and I was my own best doctor. (*She pauses, looks around at the landscape.*) Hey, you know, this is the same way we used to drive, me and my father, to visit my mother on the psych ward.

BETH: Sorry, I'm sure you could have done without that little trip down Memory Lane.

SHEILA: It's all right. You drive this route often?

BETH: Just when I visit Dad. When we were kids, though, we were on this road all the time.

SHEILA: Remember Vi's Pies? A place just off the highway, all they sold was pies, all kinds, apple, pumpkin, chocolate cream . . . that was my favorite. We used to stop there . . . before I was diagnosed, of course. And they had these funny signs all along the highway . . .

BETH: "Five miles to Vi's, pick up some pies?

SHEILA: "Vi's Pies, so nice, the whole thing or just a slice!"

BETH: "Pumpkin or peach, soon within reach!" I remember those signs. We never stopped there, because of Mom. I'm sure she wouldn't have minded, but we all felt guilty if we so much as looked at anything sweet when she was around.

SHEILA: Think the place is still there?

BETH: It must be. Most of those signs are gone, but some are still up. Let's look for them.

(*They scan both sides of the highway.*)

BETH: So, Sheila, how long since you've been out this way?

SHEILA: Years. I'm not even sure what I'm doing here now . . . not headed anywhere in particular, just taking that trip down Memory Lane, like you said. Reclaiming my emotional landscape, maybe trying to find some piece of myself I left back here.

BETH: *(She points.)* Look! There's one! A pie sign! *(Squinting.)* "Next exit leads to Vi's. Buy someone a sweet surprise!"

SHEILA: I remember that one! Come on, Beth, Honey, let's go there!

BETH: Go to Vi's? The last thing I need to do right now is eat a piece of pie. It's nearly eleven, and Dad has a feast planned for two o'clock . . . and you can be sure I'll be expected to eat plenty. Hey, Sheila, why don't you join us for Sunday dinner? Unless you really have to get right back on the road . . .

SHEILA: In a big hurry on my way to nowhere? Thanks, I'd love to have dinner with you and your family. But, listen, two o'clock is still three hours away. That's plenty of time to recover from a piece of *(She licks her lips.)* chocolate cream pie!

BETH: *(The laughs.)* Hey, you know you can't eat any pie. You're diabetic!

SHEILA: I know, Sugar Plum, no sweat. Pull over here.

BETH: Do what?

SHEILA: Pull over to the side of the road. I need to get something out of my bag in the trunk.

BETH: Can't it wait until —

SHEILA: Are you gonna pull over or what?

BETH: Geez, chill, okay? All right, I'm pulling over.

(Beth signals and pulls over. Sheila gets out of the car, goes around to the back, opens the trunk and rummages around. She returns, gets in, shuts the door and pulls out a hypodermic kit.)

SHEILA: Just need to take care of myself, Sweetie.

(Sheila lifts up her sweater and positions the needle at her midriff.)

BETH: Now? Mom always did hers in the morning . . . but where . . . what the hell are you doing?

(With eyes shut and jaws clenched, Sheila injects herself in the abdomen. Her body tenses.)

SHEILA: Oooh, watch that language, Sweet Cakes. *(She turns, looks Beth in the eye, speaks slowly and deliberately.)* Now. Listen to me. You have five minutes to get me a piece of chocolate pie or I'll go into insulin shock.

BETH: What. . . you. . . I can't believe it, you really did that, you. . . you. . . you jerk! How could you do such a stupid fucking thing! *(She pulls back onto the highway, burning rubber, reeling and speeding toward the next exit.)* Don't you know you could die right here, right here in this car? That place might not even be there. How do we know? It could have burned to the ground! It might not be open on Sunday!

(Sheila doesn't reply, just stares at the highway ahead, sweaty, pale, and tense. Beth speeds along, peels off the exit ramp and across a parking lot, comes to a screeching halt in front of Vi's front door. She reaches across Sheila and opens the passenger door for her.)

BETH: Here's your goddamn pie shop! Now get out of here, you bitch! And you can just walk to wherever it is you're going on your sick trip down Memory Lane!

(Sheila, stiff and unsteady, climbs out of the car and stumbles toward the pie shop. Beth exhales ferociously and leans forward, resting her head on the steering wheel. She looks toward the back and groans.)

BETH: Oh great, she left her bag in the trunk!

(Slowly, Beth turns into a nearby parking spot and cuts the ignition. There is a long pause, then Sheila re-emerges somewhat steadier. She spots Beth's car, walks up to it and gets in. They sit silently for a few moments, staring straight ahead.)

BETH: So, you got your piece of pie. *(Sheila nods.)* Was it worth it? *(Silence for a few moments.)* Was it even as good as you remembered?

SHEILA: *(Weak but grinning, she turns to look at Beth.)* Honey, it was just this side of Heaven. And I mean that literally. Hey, you okay? *(Pause.)* Sweetie, I forget, what time did you say your dad was expecting us?

BETH: *(She takes out a cigarette, tamps it down, lights it and blows smoke in Sheila's face.)* Two o'clock. I guess we'd better get a move on. You ready?

SHEILA: Yeah, wouldn't want to be late. There are some things you just shouldn't miss. Like a real family dinner on Sunday, Sugar. *(Beth pulls out onto the highway.)* It will be just what the doctor ordered. And Honey, it was so-o-o-o sweet of you to invite me.

WHEN THEY SPEAK OF RITA
Daisy Foote

2 Women

Scene: New Hampshire.

Rita (forty) a woman struggling to redefine herself after a failed affair and
Jeannie (seventeen) her son's girlfriend and mother of his child.

Married Rita had a brief but intense fling with Jimmy, a man much younger
than herself. When she returns to her husband, Asa, Rita finds that life has
become somewhat uncomfortable. Here, she and Jeannie talk about the past
and the future.

JEANNIE: I'm a good mother.

RITA: You know that already? Charlie's only a month old.

JEANNIE: When he was born, the minute they handed him to me, I knew I
    was meant to be a mother.

RITA: As soon as they handed him to you —

JEANNIE: Yes.

RITA: And you think that will be enough?

JEANNIE: I think it will be more than enough.

RITA: It's not too late, you can still go to college.

JEANNIE: Rita —

RITA: You could go part time, take some night courses.

JEANNIE: I don't want to.

RITA: But you were such a good student.

JEANNIE: I said I don't want to. And please stop trying to make me feel bad
    about it.

RITA: I'm not.

JEANNIE: Oh yes you are. It's like you won't be happy until I say to you, "Rita,
    I've made a big mistake. I never should have married Warren. I never
    should have had Charlie. You were right all along." I think you want me
    to be miserable.

RITA: That's not true.

JEANNIE: Then be happy for me, Rita. Be happy for me. *(A beat.)* Why don't you go to college?

RITA: Oh be quiet.

JEANNIE: I'm serious. You're always telling everyone else to go. You go.

RITA: I'm going to be forty-one next month.

JEANNIE: Oh that's so old.

RITA: I could never afford it. All we have is Asa's salary now. I even tried to get a few of my cleaning jobs back. But everyone has the same excuse, they've already hired someone else.

JEANNIE: You were gone awhile.

RITA: That's not it. No one wants me around, I go to the store to pick up some groceries or to the post office or the dump, and everyone gets so quiet. I can feel their eyes on me.

JEANNIE: It'll die down. Something else will happen, and people will start talking about that.

RITA: But I don't know if people will forget, I think they have the idea that I'm to blame for everything, not just me and Jimmy running off but Jimmy's mother killing his father and the California guy's wife —

JEANNIE: Now that's paranoid.

RITA: I'm the only one left. Everyone else is either dead, in prison or moved away. People need someone to blame.

JEANNIE: And what about Jimmy? If people are going to blame you, then why not him too?

RITA: People feel sorry for him. He has to be a father and a mother to the twins now. And people probably think I made him run away with me, that he had no say in it.

(A few beats.)

RITA: Is it true Jimmy's getting married?

JEANNIE: I heard something about it.

RITA: Who is she?

JEANNIE: Some girl he just met, I don't know anything about her.

RITA: Well I'm glad he's found someone.

JEANNIE: Are you?

RITA: Yes I am.

JEANNIE: Sometimes I can't help but wonder.

RITA: About what?

JEANNIE: If you still don't miss him.

(A beat.)
Do you?
(A few beats.)

RITA: Right after I came back here, Jimmy came to see me.

JEANNIE: He came here, to this house?

RITA: Yes. He wanted me to move in with him and the twins. He wanted me to marry him.

JEANNIE: Why did you do it, Rita? Why did you take off with him? You and Asa have been married for twenty years. You have a son. And no one, no one saw this coming. If you were so unhappy, why didn't you tell someone?

RITA: No one would have heard me.

JEANNIE: How do you know that?

RITA: I'd get up in the morning, I'd put on the coffee. I'd make breakfast. Then I'd go clean a couple of houses. I'd come home, make Asa his lunch, clean our house. Then I'd start supper, we'd watch some television. And if we were really lucky, you or Jimmy would stop by. If not, we'd go to bed and get up in the morning and start all over again. All that sameness, I couldn't stand it any more.

JEANNIE: So you take off with Jimmy Reeves?

RITA: I'd give Jimmy something to eat, he would tell me that I was the best cook in the world. I would tell him about an idea and he would actually listen. He said I was a star, a bright shining star.

JEANNIE: Oh, Rita.

RITA: You think I'm foolish.

JEANNIE: I just don't think you know how good you have it. Asa is a good husband.

RITA: I'm here, aren't I? I'm cleaning his house and baking his pies.

JEANNIE: If you really want something more than that, then do something about it.
(Picking up the paper.)
If you don't think school is possible, look in the employment section, see if anything catches your eye.

RITA: I don't have any experience.

JEANNIE: Well maybe you should go back to that catering place and tell them you'll take the job bussing tables.

RITA: Why would I want to do that?

JEANNIE: It's a place to start, Rita.
RITA: I couldn't.
JEANNIE: Why?
RITA: I just couldn't.
JEANNIE: Suit yourself.

WINNING?

Michele Forsten

3 Women

Scene: Here and now.

Susie (thirties), a woman playing cards with her mother and grandmother . . . who both happen to be deceased.

Here, Susie shares memories and insights about life with her mom and her Bubbie while seeking understanding about her partner, Annie.

GRANDMA: So, have you met anyone yet?
> *(Susie rubs her hand back and forth on her forehead in response.)*
No? You know, you're not getting any younger. I'm dead now ten years. You were getting older, even then. *(Fiddles with her cards.)* Don't you want a real home, children? And why is that Annie always in your apartment? Doesn't she have a place to live?

SUSIE: It's *our* apartment, Grandma. Remember? It's been *our* apartment for five years now.

GRANDMA: You're too generous. You'll never get a husband if you spend all your time with her.

SUSIE: Precisely the point.

MOTHER: And what's with the ring in your nose? Better you should have a ring on your finger. Right, Ma?
> *(As she says "right, ma," Susie softly says the words in unison.)*

GRANDMA: You know I can't hear you when you mumble. And straighten your shoulders, you're bent out of shape.

SUSIE: I like being bent. It's the way I am.

GRANDMA: Nothing that a good chiropractor can't cure. Your cousin Rachel, remember, she was almost on all fours. Now look at her. A doctor for a husband, three beautiful children and an extra house in the Hamptons.

SUSIE: Bubbie, stop it already! I told you 15 years ago that I was queer — remember?

GRANDMA: I thought you'd have outgrown that by now. We've come back to check up on you.

MOTHER: Remember, Susie, don't let boys take advantage of you. Kick them in the balls if they get fresh. It worked for me with that guy who tried to attack me in the hallway. I showed him. You have to make them respect you.

SUSIE: Ma, give that a rest. You told me a million times when you were alive. It's up there as my favorite bedtime tale with grandma's story about how her whole family died in the Holocaust. No wonder I'm afraid to take chances — I'm either going to be violated from the rear or shoved into a box car. Or both at the same time!

GRANDMA: *(Hits her with the cards.)* Such a mouth on you. Your jokes offend me. And stop blaming us for your unhappiness already. That Annie. She's a bad influence. That girl has such a *fahbissenah puhnem*. Next to her, a prune looks like a plum.

SUSIE: Bubbie . . .

GRANDMA: Stop complaining. And what kind of fancy schmancy doctor is Annie anyway? A PhD and she earns less than you? And by the way, what future is there in being a . . . what you call it?

SUSIE: A continuity director. I make sure that everything is the same from shot to shot in TV commercials.

MOTHER: I pleaded with you to become a teacher. It's a secure job with a good pension. But no. You'd rather go from job to job, sometimes with no work for months. Why?

SUSIE: Look, don't you have more important things to do than criticize my life? Try working toward world peace or finding a cure for breast cancer. *(Takes a deep breath.)* Breathe in calmness, breathe out stress. In, calmness; out, stress. *(Continues saying this while Grandma talks.)*

GRANDMA: We worry about you and that big sister of yours. We can't rest. We would turn over in our graves, but we're too anxious to spend any time in them. Carol and you, still not married? Oy.

SUSIE: I am visualizing a protective shield of white light around me.

MOTHER: White light? You have a few lights out, daughter, in there. *(Points to Susie's head.)* Right, Ma?

SUSIE: *(Losing it.)* Why don't you go bother Carol? Leave me alone.

MOTHER: Susie, you're whining again! We've tried. We can't get through to that sister of yours.

SUSIE: Ma, stop peeking! Next you're going to tell me how to play this hand. It was bad enough when you used to do my homework for me when I was a kid. Ever heard of boundaries?

GRANDMA: Boundaries, schmoundaries.

MOTHER: You should be grateful to have someone watching out for your best interests.

SUSIE: Get a life! Oops, too late.

MOTHER: You've never appreciated me. *(Almost crying.)* I'm your mother!

SUSIE: And *I'm* thirty-five years old. Let me make my own mistakes. Besides, you're not always right. You did marry my father, didn't you? Goddess, I can't believe you're still trying to control me. Give it a rest for a few centuries!

GRANDMA: What's this 'goddess'? You kids have no respect for your elders. That's what's wrong with the world today. We wouldn't even think of answering our parents with a mouth like that. *(Throws her cards down on the table.)* Gin! *(Picks up the cards and begins shuffling them for a new game.)*

SUSIE: Didn't you leave your mother and father in Russia to come here when you were fourteen? If I had grown up thousands of miles from mine I could be respectful, too.

MOTHER: Susie! You're being a sore loser and taking it out on us!

GRANDMA: I'm not going to play cards with you again until you take one of those ed classes to improve your game. And maybe you should try a cooking class. Between you and that girlfriend, you can't boil water to save your lives. And you never know who you might meet in a class.

SUSIE: If you hadn't taken all your recipes to the grave, maybe I'd have a larger repertoire of dishes. Everytime I asked you how to make something, you had an excuse why you couldn't tell me. And, I'm not looking to 'meet' anyone. Since you're both such know-it-alls, how come you don't know that Annie and I are lovers? Hello, we're in a committed relationship!

(Grandma drops cards she is shuffling on the table.)

Or is that one of the pleasures of heaven, or wherever you are, that you only see what you want to see?

MOTHER: This is what you went to college for, to sling insults right and left? We're not going to visit you any more if you act like this. Right, Ma?

SUSIE: Still running everything by Grandma for approval. Stop with the guilt trip! Is this what I have to look forward to through eternity? I'm sick of both of you seeing me as a loser. The fact that I support myself, have an intelligent, interesting partner, and loyal friends means nothing. You couldn't care less whether I'm happy or not. *(Throws her cards and jumps up.)* Well, I'm not playing your game any more! Go do something useful, like haunt the Vatican. Go on!

GRANDMA: Susie, wait, sit down.

SUSIE: *(Still standing.)* Why should I?

GRANDMA: *(Shuffling the cards.)* Why not? You have something better to do?

SUSIE: Oh, I can think of a few more pleasant things . . . like, lying down on a bed of nails.

GRANDMA: *(Cuts cards.)* Nails? So now you're a big martyr like Jesus Christ?

SUSIE: Being in the closet all these years so I wouldn't upset dad, Aunt Celia and the rest of the family . . . Yeah, I'm up there with the best of them.

MOTHER: I don't get it.

SUSIE: Imagine if you had to hide that you are . . . I mean were . . . Jewish.

MOTHER: Don't mix oranges with apples.

SUSIE: Excuse me, there is a connection. The pink triangle . . . gays went up the chimneys with the Jews in World War Two.

GRANDMA: Okay, okay. Stop with the history lesson. I get it. But why blame us for the . . . the way you are?

SUSIE: That's not it. I want you to accept me as a lesbian. Remember, Bubbie, after Ma died, you kept asking me why I wasn't popular with the boys?

GRANDMA: So? *(Puts more money in the pot.)* I raise you one.

SUSIE: So I answered that I *was* popular . . . with the girls. And you just dropped the subject. Not only that, you never bugged me about dating again . . . until now.

MOTHER: We come back, we see you're still not married. We . . .

GRANDMA: I thought you'd have outgrown that . . . that life by now.

SUSIE: This is hopeless! *(To Grandma.)* There's an expression that AIDS activists use, "Silence equals Death." It took years for me to see that your silence was as bad as your dating spiel. It made me afraid to come out to anyone else in the family.

GRANDMA: A nice Jewish boy would have fixed everything. Now, from what you're saying, I see it's too late. Gin.

SUSIE: *(Shuffling the cards.)* Listen to me. I needed your approval. I wanted you to hock me about when I was going to find a girlfriend, a lover! I wanted you to love me the way I was. Ignoring me like you did hurts me to this day.

GRANDMA: It's a good thing I'm dead or this conversation would kill me. *(Cuts the cards.)*

SUSIE: *(Sarcastically.)* Let me tell you something that'll make you happy. Thanks to me and Annie, Carol is getting married next week.

MOTHER: Susie, is this another one of your lousy jokes?

(Susie emphatically shakes her head 'no.')

GRANDMA: I'm so happy! Who's your sister's lucky man?

SUSIE: Adam. He's my *woman's* best friend.

MOTHER: We've seen him for years at your house. Funny, we never thought of him for Carol.

GRANDMA: A nice boy. So, he's not a big shot in business making all the gelt. That boy's got a good soul. I thought he was keeping company with Annie. But you, Susie, you finally got it through our heads today that you and Annie are, you know.

SUSIE: I raise you, a dollar. *You* know. Say it, Bubbie.

GRANDMA: An item, a couple, each other's love slave. You happy now?

SUSIE: Ecstatic.

GRANDMA: So how is it that they are going to be Mr. and Mrs.?

SUSIE: How come you don't know these things? I thought you hover around, checking up on us.

MOTHER: We've been away, at an intergalactical bingo marathon. Grandma was one of our coordinators. She's as big a *macher* over there as she was over here.

GRANDMA: They like it when I call the numbers. No one has trouble hearing me. *(Puts more money in the pot.)* I raise you two.

MOTHER: I'm out.

SUSIE: Bingo? Are you sure you weren't assigned to hell?

GRANDMA: So how did they get together, Ms. Smarty Pants?

SUSIE: Well, after a few lukewarm encounters at our house, they met quite accidentally at Radio Shack one Saturday night. Carol was there to replace her lap-top and Adam needed to get one. He didn't know the first thing about what to buy and asked Carol for advice.

GRANDMA: That's not very hot and heavy to me.

MOTHER: Hardly the stuff of romance.

SUSIE: Look, you want to know what happened or not?

GRANDMA: Yeah, but how about making it fast? Or we'll be late for the Scrabble Tournament.

SUSIE: All right. Adam asked her to help him set up the computer and teach him how to use Lotus. Well, you know how generous Carol can be.

MOTHER: A little too generous over the years with her private parts, if you ask me, right Ma?

SUSIE: They spent some afternoons together doing the computer stuff. Then he took her to a fancy restaurant to thank her for the trouble.

GRANDMA: A little food, a little wine and my Carol-a gave away her goodies, just like that?

SUSIE: No, Bubbie. See, they were both tiptoeing around on eggshells. Both of them had recently been dumped. I guess their mutual interest in computers made them throw caution to the wind. Or something like that. Anyway, Carol ended up proposing to him on line.

GRANDMA: On-line? The women were lined up to grab him? Feh! What happened to the man asking the woman to marry him? *Oy vayz mir,* I see where your women's lib has taken things. Right into the toilet!

SUSIE: Bubbie, chill. It wasn't like that at all. Oh, I'm tired of talking. They're getting married. Isn't that enough for you?

MOTHER: But will it last long enough for me to see some grandchildren?

SUSIE: Grandchildren? They're getting a pet pig. That'll keep them hopping for now.

GRANDMA: A pig? In a Jewish home? *Oy, guttenu.*

SUSIE: Bubbie! Can't you, once, be positive? Try.

GRANDMA: Okay, okay. I'm kvelling that our Carol-a is going to be a Mrs., pig or no pig.

MOTHER: I wish I were alive to dance at their wedding.

GRANDMA: Alive or dead, let's boogie.

(Music comes on and Grandma and Mother leap up and shake their booties for a couple of seconds. Susie closes her eyes and shakes her head as if she can't believe what's happening. The music stops and they sit down again and resume the card game, as if they had never gotten up.)

SUSIE: And to think, they're getting married on our anniversary.

MOTHER: Anniversary?

SUSIE: Annie's and mine. The day we first slept together. The date we celebrate as our anniversary.

GRANDMA: Oy. So, what is it, your fourth?

SUSIE: Sixth, Bubbie.

MOTHER: Time really flies when you're dead. Right, Ma?

SUSIE: We're as good as married. It's time you took us seriously. Get it?

GRANDMA: *Nu,* if you're happy, we're happy. *(Sighs.)* So what if Annie's Catholic and a she?

SUSIE: Do you mean it? Or are you just saying that because you're so thrilled about Carol? *(Doesn't let them respond.)* Whatever the reason, I have one thing to say to both of you.

GRANDMA AND MOTHER: *(In unison.)* What?

SUSIE: Gin!

(Grandma pinches her cheek as the lights go down.)

PERMISSION ACKNOWLEDGMENTS